The Prost...

CW00949766

K. SURANGKHANANG

The Prostitute

Translated from the Thai with an Introduction by
DAVID SMYTH

KUALA LUMPUR
OXFORD UNIVERSITY PRESS
OXFORD SINGAPORE NEW YORK
1994

Oxford University Press

Oxford New York
Athens Auckland Bangkok Bombay
Calcutta Cape Town Dar es Salaam Delhi
Florence Hong Kong Istanbul Karachi
Kuala Lumpur Madras Madrid Melbourne
Mexico City Nairobi Paris Singapore
Taipei Tokyo Toronto

and associated companies in
Berlin Ibadan

Oxford is a trade mark of Oxford University Press

Published in the United States
by Oxford University Press, New York

British Library Cataloguing in Publication Data
Data available

Library of Congress Cataloging-in-Publication Data
K. Surangkhanang, 1911–
[Ying khon chua. English]
The prostitute/K. Surangkhanang; translated from the Thai with
an introduction by David Smyth.
p.   cm—(Oxford in Asia paperbacks)
ISBN 967 65 3079 4
1. Prostitution—Thailand—Fiction. I. Smyth, David, 1954–
II. Title. III. Series.
PL4209.K24Y5613   1994
891.9′133—dc20
94-28440
CIP

The Translator and Publishers have made every effort to trace
the original copyright of this book, but with no success.
Anyone claiming copyright should write to the
Publishers at the address given below

Typeset by Indah Photosetting Centre Sdn. Bhd., Malaysia
Printed by KHL Printing Co. Pte. Ltd., Singapore
Published by Oxford University Press,
19–25, Jalan Kuchai Lama, 58200 Kuala Lumpur, Malaysia

Introduction

The fact that the author gave the book this title was, I think,
right. Of course, it may make some people rush out and buy
it, in the hope that it will be what is called a 'pornographic'
story. If that is so, they will be disappointed because there are
no obscene or dirty bits in it at all. But some people, fearing
that it is a 'pornographic' book, will not buy it, which is an
even greater shame because they will miss the chance to read
a gripping story.[1]

IN 1937 a young lady from a well-to-do family offered the
manuscript of her newly completed novel to a number of
Bangkok publishers. It was called *Ying khon chua* or *The
Prostitute*. The idea for this, her third full-length novel, had
first come to Kanha Watanaphat when, as a schoolgirl, she
observed the comings and goings at a brothel opposite her
home, behind Wat Somanat. One day, she resolved, she
would describe in a novel the tragic lives of the women who
lived there.

Kanha was born on 26 February 1911 in Thonburi, the
eldest of three children. Her father, Phra Suriyaphakdi, was a
high-ranking civil servant. She was educated at St Francis
Xavier Convent and Rachini Bon schools and on completing
her secondary education became a teacher of Thai at the
exclusive Rachini Lang School. In January 1936 she married
the journalist and writer, Puan Buranasinlapin, and within a

year, resigned from her teaching post in order to devote her energies to writing full time.[2]

No longer restricted by the expectations imposed on her as a teacher, Kanha set to work on *The Prostitute*. Accompanied by her husband, she visited a brothel in order to observe conditions at first hand. For one of the main characters, she drew on a true story a colleague had told her about a wife forced to turn to prostitution to feed herself after her husband's imprisonment. The novel took just three months to complete.

Publishers were shocked and rejected the work immediately. The title alone was sufficient to convince them that the content was immoral and pornographic; and they were scandalized that a young woman of Kanha's background should be writing such a book. 'Some,' Kanha recalled, 'even went as far as to say, "As a woman teacher, it would be better for you to be writing cookery books or manuals on childcare rather. Why on earth did you write that story about prostitutes?"'[3] Kanha had little option but to publish the book herself.

In her introduction to the first edition, Kanha struggles to conceal her irritation at publishers and friends who questioned her choice of subject-matter. 'Why should I have to write a story about people who are always praised for being good,' she demands, 'when goodness, even if it is difficult to find among prostitutes, has not yet completely disappeared?'[4] *The Prostitute* was written both 'out of a feeling of sympathy and compassion' and as a challenge to conventional beliefs that such women must be totally bad. 'High-class women,' Kanha adds provocatively, 'may have base minds just as low-class women may be noble-minded.'[5] She concludes by sarcastically thanking those who warned her against writing the book and declaring defiantly, 'I have done what I have done and I dare to take responsibility for it, fully and happily.'[6]

The Prostitute tells the story of Reun, a country girl, who is seduced by a sophisticated young pimp from Bangkok and then tricked into prostitution. While working in a brothel, she meets and falls in love with Wit, a young man from an aristocratic background. But after vowing to rescue Reun and marry her, Wit disappears. Unknown to him, she is pregnant with his child. Samorn, another prostitute, helps her to escape from the brothel, and together they struggle to raise the child in a rented house. When Samorn falls sick and dies, Reun is forced back into prostitution and entrusts her daughter to the care of a childless couple. As her own health deteriorates and death approaches, Reun by chance meets Wit, who, although now married, agrees to take responsibility for raising the child.

The novel created a considerable stir in Thai literary circles. To make prostitutes the central characters in the story and then portray them in a more favourable light than apparently respectable members of society was controversial enough; that the author was herself a young woman from a respectable and sheltered background made the work all the more remarkable. The plot itself follows the conventions of the popular romantic fiction of the day, but the author's lively style and realistic portrayal of Reun's exploitation at the hands of employers, rent-collectors, money-lenders, and child-minders reflect the author's serious intention and raise the work above the purely sentimental.

Unusually for the time, *The Prostitute* went into a second edition of 2,000 copies within the same year. A positive review by the British-educated Prince Chula Chakrabongse helped to secure its reputation and this was reprinted in all later editions of the novel.[7] A third edition appeared in 1941 and a fourth in 1949. It was finally made into a film in 1958 after Kanha had refused earlier requests to dramatize the story.[8] The most recent reprint was in 1988 as part of a major reissue of her novels.[9] Today, *The Prostitute* is generally acknowledged by scholars of the Thai novel as one of the major early works in the Thai canon.

In the years that followed the publication of *The Prostitute*, K. Surangkhanang became a household name in the Thai literary world, a popular and prolific writer of novels, short stories, and magazine articles, as well as being the owner of several publishing companies and a regular newspaper columnist. Her most famous novels include *Ban sai thong* (1950), *Potchaman Sawangwong* (1950), *Dok fa* (1953), *Kulap daeng* (1955), and *Khemerin-Inthira* (1959). In all, she wrote over forty novels and almost a hundred short stories, several of which have been made into films or television plays. In 1986 she was honoured with the title 'National Artist in Literary Arts (The Novel)'.

1. Prince Chula Chakrabongse, 'Wichan ru'ang "Ying khon chua" khong K. Surangkhanang' [Review of K. Surangkhanang's 'The Prostitute'], in K. Surangkhanang, *Ying khon chua* [The Prostitute], 4th edn., Bangkok: Khochittamet, 1949, pp. 3–10.

2. Puan Buranasinlapin later changed the family name to Buranapakorn. After his death, Kanha remarried and took her second husband's surname, Khiangsiri. The pen-name 'K. Surangkhanang' derived from a Thai classical verse form, *kap surangkhanang*.

3. K. Surangkhanang, *Ying khon chua*, p. 13.

4. Ibid., pp. 17–18.

5. Ibid., p. 23.

6. Ibid., pp. 23–4. The author concludes the Introduction to the fourth edition by describing prostitutes as 'unfortunate younger sisters' and dedicating the book to them (ibid., pp. 15–16).

7. Prince Chula Chakrabongse took a great interest in the literary scene of the day and was eager to encourage young writers. It appears that his 'review' was actually published in the first edition.

8. K. Surangkhanang, *Ying khon chua*, pp. 14–15. The author reveals that she had failed to reach an agreement over film rights because she insisted on a half-share in the profits which would be donated to a welfare

scheme for prostitutes. An attempt to stage a dramatized version shortly after the end of World War II foundered for a rather different reason, when the leading lady in the troupe said she would rather die than play a prostitute!

9. To commemorate the occasion of K. Surangkhanang being honoured as a 'National Artist' in 1986, Odeon Store republished many of her most popular novels in a paperback series.

A Note on Sources

Little has been written about K. Surangkhanang in English. Sources used in the preparation of this Introduction include:

Bunsi Phinyathinan, *Kansu'ksa choeng wikhro nawaniyai khong K. Surangkhanang* [An Analytical Study of K. Surangkhanang's Novels], MA thesis, Department of Thai, Graduate School, Chulalongkorn University, 1984.

K. Surangkhanang, *Ying khon chua* [The Prostitute], 4th edn., Bangkok: Khochittamet, 1949.

Prakat Watcharaphon, *Nak khian ... nak nangsu'phim* [Writers ... journalists], Bangkok: Odeon Store, 1984, pp. 78–85.

Sathian Chanthimathon, *Khon khian nangsu* [Writers], Bangkok: Praphansan, 1979, pp. 100–18.

Suan nangsu [Book Garden], Vol. 12, Bangkok: Dok ya, 1992.

Suphanni Warathon, *Prawat kan praphan nawaniyai thai* [History of the Thai Novel], Bangkok: Munnitthi khrongkan tamra sangkhomsat lae manut-sayasat, 1976.

Trisin Bunkhachon, *Nawaniyai kap sangkhom thai (2475–2500)* [The Novel and Thai Society (1932–1957)], Bangkok: Sangsan, 1980.

A Note on the Translation

In translating this novel, I have endeavoured to stick as closely to the Thai original as possible. To avoid unnecessary repetitions, however, a few very minor abridgements have been made. I am, as ever, indebted to my wife, Somsong, for her patience in dealing with my many queries. Errors of fact or translation are, of course, my sole responsibility.

One

A huge lamp swept an arc of bright light before it as it approached from a distance. Behind the light, people standing some way away would, in the first instance, see just a dark shadow with sparks shooting into the darkness like fireworks. Eventually, however, it would become apparent to the eye that it was an engine pulling a long row of carriages. The sound of metal wheels against the rails and the echo of the pistons pumping reverberated in the air. A crewman sounded the whistle and gradually the train slowed down. A sign that read 'Hua Hin' was weakly illuminated for a moment and then plunged into darkness once more as the engine hauled its carriages along the station platform. The buzz of conversation could be heard from carriages where the lights were on. Some passengers drowsily poked their heads out of the windows. People starting their journey from the station were preparing to board, while those getting off were fussing around with their arms full. Nine o'clock was the time when the Bangkok–Padang Besar express arrived, bringing with it all the usual hustle and bustle.

A young man of medium height and slender build, dressed in travelling attire which was clearly not very fashionable, attracted the attention of several of the passengers leaning out of the windows. As he mounted the steps of the second-class carriage, he turned and reached out a hand towards a uniformed employee from the Hua Hin Hotel, who swiftly passed him a smallish travelling bag. Some people even smiled to themselves when they saw the young hotel employee cheerfully bow his head in respect before holding out a hand to accept the banknote with which the man tipped him.

As the train moved out of the station, the young man with the bag opened the glass door and entered the carriage. By the light shining from the ceiling, it was possible for the two or three passengers sitting facing the carriage door to see his swarthy face quite clearly. From his appearance and demeanour, together with the fact that he had a hotel employee accompany him to the station and had tipped him, it was obvious that he was rather well-off. His broad face showed a good-natured disposition but his rather nervous manner indicated that he had been away from the city for at least two or three years.

The shaking of the train as it gathered speed along the rails made the bag sway unsteadily in his hands. Murmuring his apologies, the man made his way to an empty seat almost at the end of the carriage. He pushed his bag under the seat and heaved a sigh of relief. He took out a handkerchief and mopped the sweat from his brow and cheeks, beneath his nose, and around the top of his neck. He then looked around at his fellow passengers. The man in front of him was a fat Chinese who looked as if he was a merchant. Although he was sitting up, his eyes were tightly closed and he appeared to be snoring softly. The young man turned his gaze to the right. Two Indians with bushy moustaches were chattering away noisily in a language he did not understand. Quite sure that he had caught a whiff of butter, he turned round, rubbing his nose as he did so, to have a look at the last passenger. He could tell immediately from the green uniform that this was a soldier. He saw three shiny stars on his shoulder and the man's carefully combed hair as he leaned forward reading. He turned back, feeling rather pleased that one of his fellow passengers was an army captain. Almost immediately, another thought struck him. He had seen this officer before. He sat frowning, his head between his hands, as if deep in thought. He turned round again suddenly, leaning forward so much that his shadow startled the captain. The officer looked up from his newspaper to meet the young man's gaze as casually as he could. The moment their eyes met, they both cried out simultaneously.

'Charn!'

'Damrong!'

'It can't be!'

'It is you, you old rascal!'

On a long overnight journey, a familiar face is always welcome, especially if it happens to belong to a friend. The young man was so pleased he almost jumped over the seat while the captain threw his newspaper aside and got up, shouting something incomprehensible. It was only after they had clasped hands in pleasure that they regained their composure. As they did so, they became aware of the two Indians staring at them in astonishment and irritation and the Chinese man looking thoroughly bewildered. Captain Charn indicated that they should lower their voices to a whisper.

'Damrong, I'm so pleased to see you, I'm forgetting myself. I was thinking we were back in the beer halls and not on a train.'

Damrong looked over his shoulder and then turned back and smiled. 'Where we met four or five years ago,' he said, relaxing and sitting down. He looked up thoughtfully. 'How many years was it actually? Four. Yes, it must have been four years. So where are you going now?' With his manly bearing, strong shoulders, and full face, his friend had scarcely changed.

'I've got fifteen days' official leave, so I thought I'd go home and see my parents.' People overhearing this may not have understood where Captain Charn came from, but Damrong and Charn had been at school together and Damrong had often teased him about speaking the southern dialect.

'How about you? I heard you were in business in Songkhla. What are you doing up here? You got on at Hua Hin, didn't you?'

Damrong nodded. 'Yes. I thought I'd take two or three days off before plodding on,' he said, with a look of determination on his face. A second later he changed the topic of conversation. 'How are things in Bangkok? Which of all those unattached young ladies are still unattached? Or have they all been snapped up by now?'

'Only a few have become "Mrs". These days they're not so hasty to take the plunge as when you were in Bangkok,' said Charn with a laugh as he took out a cigarette and slipped it between his lips. He reached into his trouser pocket, but Damrong was quicker, handing his friend a match from his jacket pocket, although his face showed he was surprised by Charn's news.

'All I'd heard was that the fashion in clothes had changed. I didn't realize that kind of thing had changed, too. So none of them have got married then? I suppose that includes Choamchai, Niramon, and Ladda.'

'Apparently, only Niramon has joined the ranks of the wedded. No one else apart from her.' Charn paused to light his cigarette and then tossed the used match out of the window. 'Why do people get married when it's just about the same whether you're married or not? Or perhaps it's a bit better if you're not, because then some foolish young fellow will come along and fall in love with you.'

'That's true. I hadn't fully appreciated what you said,' Damrong admitted. 'I'm becoming a hermit. The mere mention of society news is enough to make me feel sick,' he added, screwing up his face as he spoke.

The captain roared with delight. 'You can feel sick for two different reasons. Feeling sick because you've been starving for a long time is one. And eating too much is another. Which is it in your case?'

Damrong smiled in embarrassment at his friend's teasing. 'Probably the latter rather than the former. What about you, though? Back then, you were involved with the older sister of that good-looking kid. Now, what was his name? I can't remember. What was it? The fellow whose older sister you were keen on. A bright-looking and rather self-assured fellow. Your wallet was almost empty by the time you'd got him to be your go-between.'

Charn allowed Damrong to finish reminiscing. 'Wit,' he said casually. 'That's the fellow you're talking about. He now happens to be uncle to my children.'

Damrong's face registered his surprise. 'Good grief!' he exclaimed loudly. 'Is that so?' When he saw from Charn's expression that it was true, his surprise gave way to pleasure. 'Allow me to congratulate you. You go forgetting yourself for just a moment and you become a father. I'm beginning to feel old already. How many children have you got?'

Charn raised his index finger and middle finger by way of reply.

'Not bad,' Damrong murmured.

They were both silent for a moment. Then Damrong rose and told Charn he was going to the buffet car. He returned about ten minutes later, followed by a steward carrying a tray with two glasses of whisky and a bottle of soda. The steward placed the tray down carefully, removed the top from the soda bottle, and then left. Damrong poured the soda into the first glass of whisky and passed it to Charn, taking the remaining glass himself.

'It's to stop me feeling drowsy,' Damrong said. 'Whenever I go on a train, I can never sleep. How about you?'

The captain nodded in agreement. He raised his glass to drink but took only a small sip before putting it down. He pointed to a pile of books on the next seat. 'I have to carry about ten books with me.'

Just then, the train raced past a small station. Damrong stuck his head out to take a look and then withdrew it as if he had just thought of something he wanted to say. 'How's your children's uncle, then, these days? He must be a young man now. When you were a lieutenant, he was in eighth grade. There was something about him, you know.'

'Whatever it is,' said Charn, 'old Wit's like we were at that age, only he's a thousand times better. Kids these days are brighter than we were. They're better than us in every way. They don't have to go out and work. Their good fortune just seems to increase. Now he's becoming a favourite of the girls. There's something about him, as you say. Everyone likes Wit. He's a good conversationalist, he's knowledgeable—in fact, he's good at everything. I couldn't compete with him. Luang Phaisan, who used to be well-known in society, seems to have dropped right out of sight because he was overshadowed by Wit.'

'He's that good, is he?' said Damrong in wonder. 'He must be quite a character. In those days, there was no one to match Luang Phaisan either at sports or for charm. He was all right with the ladies, too.'

'When it comes to the ladies,' Charn interrupted, 'old Wit's not bad either. But there's something peculiar about him. He doesn't like the nice girls. He'd much rather spend his time with the not-so-nice ones. His elder sister confided in me that Wit went to her on the quiet to ask for her help in bringing a prostitute to live in his home.'

'And did your wife help?' Damrong asked, leaning forward and pricking up his ears. This was getting interesting.

'Who's going to help? No matter how hard someone tries to make you feel pity and sympathy, you can't. Chao Khun Adithep's family is an old and well-established family, and my mother-in-law's, even more so. Huh! You can't even speak in a loud voice. So common,' said Charn, dragging out the last word. 'So how are they ever going to accept a prostitute into their home as a daughter-in-law? Merely knowing her son has been frequenting brothels has been enough to send her into fits of fainting. They couldn't get round to the doctor's quickly enough.'

'Does your mother-in-law know that her son has fallen for a prostitute?' Damrong asked.

'She didn't at first. She was looking for a wealthy daughter-in-law. But Wit didn't like the girl his mother found him. He was put under such pressure that he just went off the rails, visiting brothels. Almost immediately, there was trouble. There was such a fuss that I couldn't even face her, because Wit was fool enough to tell his mother that he was in love with a prostitute and that he had been to see her many times and was thinking of bringing the girl home to live with him. Strange, isn't it? Nice girls with plenty of money he doesn't like. Instead, he runs off and falls head-over-heels in love with a prostitute. Now wherever he goes, there has to be someone keeping an eye on him. My mother-in-law is afraid he'll be off to the brothel.'

'Why try to keep tabs on him? It's a waste of time. If it's not that place, it'll be another,' Damrong remarked sympathetically. 'If you can't go today, there's still tomorrow and lots of day-after-tomorrows. Can you keep a man penned in the same way as a girl?'

Charn nodded. 'Right. That's the way I see it, too. So I went and spoke to my mother-in-law and explained that tying down a young man of Wit's age wouldn't do any good. On the contrary, it would cause him to run wild whenever he got the opportunity. It would be far better to go easy with him and besides, it isn't appropriate to tie a man down like this. Better to let him have responsibility for his own life and then he'd learn what was good and what was bad. Everything in life is an education. Going to prostitutes is one of the lessons.'

'You're absolutely right,' Damrong agreed. 'Did his mother see it that way?'

'Huh!' Charn shook his head wearily. 'Not a chance. Instead she claimed that I was one of Wit's friends and that it had probably been I who had taken him out and introduced him to the whore-houses.'

'Well, there you are,' Damrong chuckled. 'I'll bet you protested your innocence loudly enough.'

'"Mother", I said, "in these kinds of matters, you don't need to be taught. It's just something you know for yourself, and see for yourself, all on your own, if you're a man." Isn't that so? Who taught us? No one. It was all on our own. And it's not just us I'm talking about. Lots of monks who have reached ninth or tenth grade tire of the yellow robe and leave the monkhood. Who teaches them? Some of them have studied the dharma ever since they first became novices and have no comprehension of the word "woman". Then the moment they get the scent . . . wow! Say no more!'

'You're looking down on religion,' Damrong chided softly.

'No,' Charn countered. 'I'm not looking down on religion. Religion is one thing. People are another. Religion is something good, something pure and untainted. Religion is a pillar for people to cling to. But people can be good and bad. If they're not bad today, who knows, they might be tomorrow.' He spread his hands and shrugged his shoulders as he spoke. 'Lust occurs in people, not in religion. Can you be so sure that your venerable monks have transcended their senses of form, taste, smell, hearing, and touch? If that were the case, my friend, every temple would be full of genuine monks. There wouldn't be monks reporting to the authorities that their quarters had been broken into and their bowls taken; there wouldn't be monks surrounded by flocks of female devotees, both young and old. To take an example, there's that monk—what's his name?—at the temple next to your house. Girls like going there to have their fortunes told.'

'You mean Maha Heng?'

'That's the one. He's practising as a fortune-teller. He'll ask your date of birth and then predict a partner. He sits there cross-legged in a quite unbearable way, waggling his feet and winking with a horrible leer on his face.'

'That's enough,' said Damrong. 'You're a bit too negative. People who believe that all monks follow the precepts faithfully would be cursing you if they could hear you.' As he spoke, he looked round suspiciously to the front and behind.

'Well, it's true,' the captain chuckled, getting up to stretch so as to avoid cramp.

'I wasn't arguing about the truth of what you were saying, but truth can cause offence these days. Let's drop the subject of religion. I'm still intrigued by what you were telling me about Wit. You were saying your mother-in-law had to find someone to watch his every step and that he couldn't go anywhere. So what happened next?' Damrong asked, taking a last sip from his whisky.

'You're like a little kid wanting to hear a story,' said Charn. 'Why do you ask about the restrictions on Wit? In my personal opinion, they're pointless. Now, why did my mother-in-law do that?' He raised a hand and pointed a hand directly at Damrong, stressing his words as he spoke. 'Because people have an instinct to roam. You don't have to limit their area or age. Therefore there's nothing odd about Wit going out anywhere. The only odd thing is the places he goes to.' As he finished, he laughed. Not a laugh of amusement but a laugh reflecting some deeper insight into the mind. The sound was drowned by the thunder of the train's iron wheels reverberating at regular intervals.

*   *   *

At this point of the story, you may think that if it is not the army captain who is the main character in this story, then it must be his friend. However, that is not the case. Yet each shares a connection with the main character, who, even as his praises are being sung, is stepping out of a taxi which had pulled up in the rain in the Phraeng Sanphasat district of Bangkok. He takes out a 1-baht note, hands it to the driver, and then walks briskly through the rain, past the Chinese grocery shop and into the darkness, without a backward glance at the car which delivered him and is now gradually disappearing.

Two

HE stepped over the puddle in the middle of the road as if he was in a great hurry, almost breaking into a run as he went. Wrapped up under a dark grey raincoat, he made his way towards the fence that surrounded the rather old, pale blue, two-storey house. He pulled his raincoat more tightly round himself with his left hand as he went up to the gate. Standing there, he looked up at the narrow window which was wide open. His sharp features were clearly visible by the light from the window. Drops of rain trickled down his cheeks and hung on his thin lips. Despite his slender physique, he had the appearance of a man at once strong and gentle.

Inside, he could hear people talking. But they did not hear him, because, once more, the rain falling on the eaves of the house drowned out the sound of his banging against the gate. He banged again, harder than before, so that his hand hurt. Then he saw a girl's hand slowly raising the old bamboo blind at the front of the upstairs veranda. She was wearing a loose red camisole and her hair was in a mess. She leaned out and yelled, 'Who's that knocking?'

'It's me,' he shouted back. 'Open up quickly. I'm drenched.'

The gateway where the young man was standing was not so dark as to make it impossible to see anything. There was still a dim light shining from the side of the road, sufficient for the girl just to be able to make out that it was someone who had often been here before.

'Who's *me*? Is that you, Wit?' she yelled out, above the noise of the rain, just to be sure.

'Yes,' he shouted back abruptly. 'I suppose you think it's all right, standing out here in the pouring rain. Get someone to come and open the gate.'

The girl gave a shrill laugh and took her hand away from the bamboo blind. She went back inside and a moment later there was the sound of the door being opened downstairs. A boy of about thirteen, in black school shorts and a white T-shirt, ran out into the rain to unbolt the gate for him. The young man gave the boy a friendly slap around the head and murmured his thanks. He went upstairs and took off his black leather shoes, which were soaking wet and covered with mud, and placed them out of sight by the veranda wall. Then he walked into the room on the right, which had been arranged for receiving visitors. Inside the room, rattan chairs, which were neither old nor new, were arranged around a rattan table on which there was a white tablecloth. On top stood a glass jug and two or three glasses. In the enamel ashtray were several old cigarette butts and one that was still smouldering, indicating that it had only just been discarded. On one side of the room was a rattan sofa, large enough to seat two or three people, and directly opposite, a dressing-table, complete with comb, powder, and a bottle of perfume.

As soon as she saw who it was, the middle-aged woman sitting in the adjoining room called out a welcoming greeting. She was about forty-seven and rather fat, with a coarse complexion; she was wearing a red, floral sarong and a cream-coloured *pa taep*.

'Dear me, I wondered who on earth it was. I didn't realize it was you. I heard 'Win shouting out to the kid to open the gate, but when I asked who it was, I didn't catch the answer. Come on in and make yourself at home,' she said, inviting him into the room where she was sitting. The room was bare except for a single mat, on which she sat, chewing betel. Hung up untidily on the wall were girls' camisoles and a boy's shirts.

He smiled at her greeting. Tossing his hat down on the sofa, he took off his raincoat and shook it vigorously before spreading it out over one of the chairs. He looked down at his French silk jacket and black silk trousers, and seeing they were only slightly wet, he entered the room and sat down on a mat immediately in front of the woman.

'How are things, then, Ba? Are you keeping well?'

'Yes, I can't complain. How about you? I haven't seen you just lately. You haven't been round for several days.' She brought out the betel bowl. 'Do take your jacket off. Anyone would think you'd never been here before.'

Wit laughed drily, offering his excuses as he unbuttoned his jacket. 'There's been a merit-making ceremony at home, so I couldn't get away. Well, I could have, but it wouldn't have looked very good, would it?'

'Child!' cried the woman, calling to her son, the same boy who had earlier opened the gate for Wit and who was now sitting reading in the lounge. 'Come and hang the gentleman's jacket up. There, give it to the boy, now.'

'Please don't bother, Ba, there's no need to get up. There's no need, young man,' he said, raising a hand in protest as he saw the boy closing his book. 'You carry on with your reading. I can hang it up by myself.' He got up and went and hung his jacket up against the wall and then went over to where the boy was sitting reading. He stood in front of the boy and patted him on the head again. 'What are you reading?' he asked, kindly.

'An English book,' the boy replied, looking up. Just then, his mother got up, and having adjusted her upper garment, she emerged from the room where she had been sitting. As she stood there with them, her face was filled with pride that her son could read English. Wit asked to see the book and the boy handed it to him. 'You're on this one already, are you, young man? Mmm. That's jolly good. Jolly good.' His praise was sincere, for the book he was holding was a fifth- or sixth-grade text. The boy was only about thirteen, so if he could cope with a fifth- or sixth-grade book, he was certainly no fool.

'Your son's not bad, you know. Do all you can for him. And you, young man,' he added, patting him encouragingly on the shoulder, 'keep at it with the books, right?'

'He's bright,' said the woman. 'Has been ever since he was small. I'd like him to finish eighth grade so he could be a teacher, but he doesn't want to. He wants to be a lawyer. I suppose I'll have to let him do what he wants. He's my only son. If it were a daughter, of course, I couldn't care less.'

The boy looked up and stared at him rather shyly as his mother praised him. Wit stole a clear look at his face. What Ba Taht, the owner of these premises, had just said, made an immediate impression upon him. Whoever this Ba Taht woman was, and whatever her occupation, when it came to her son, she loved him, and intended that he should study, in the hope that he might become a teacher or a lawyer. Since her son had turned out to be so bright and was polite and well-mannered, too, in the future he might well become a teacher, passing on knowledge to the nation's citizens in their dozens. Or he might become an eminent lawyer. Or perhaps even the Supreme Patriarch, if his thoughts inclined in that particular direction. And who knows just how many of the great, the good, and the wise, among whom Ba Taht's son would one day be numbered, built their lives of virtue with money gained from the toil and sweat of those who did something cursed and despised and were virtually shunned by the rest of society? And when it came to Ba Taht herself, it was quite clear that while she loved her own child and wanted the best for him, when it came to other people's children, whom she had lured away and moulded into playthings for men, there was no question of kindness or compassion, whatsoever. Her aim was money, the money which those poor women had to earn for her so that she could bring up her son and support him in his studies. But why should he criticize Ba Taht, when that was the kind of person she was?

Wit, who had been standing in silence for some time, looked round and began to grumble loudly. 'Well, where have all your girls got to, then? Have they got visitors upstairs, or something? I've been here ages, and I haven't seen a single one show her face.'

'They're upstairs. I think only 'Win's got a visitor.' Ba Taht lumbered into the room where the staircase was and yelled up in unceremonious fashion. ''Sert! 'Mai! 'Laem! Samorn! Reun! Where on earth have you all got to? We've had a visitor here all this time, yet you didn't come down.' She came back rather breathlessly and sat down in a chair. 'You see, that's the way it is. I'm exhausted. Child, take your book and go and read in that room,' she added, sending her son off to read somewhere else.

'Looks as though things are a bit quiet at the moment,' the young man said. He could make out the sound of girls giggling as they tramped down the stairs.

'It's the end of the month, you know,' said Ba Taht. 'Ah, they're down now. But what are they hanging around for now? They're a disgrace, they are, this lot. Always putting on airs. It's a good job it's you, you know. Otherwise they'd be really fed up.' She turned round and called the girls crowding behind the curtain in the doorway to come out.

Wit laughed good-humouredly. He stared quite openly through the curtain to see if he could catch a glimpse of the one girl he wanted to see. 'Come on out, then. Come and have a bit of a laugh. I'm not exactly a stranger, you know. In fact, I've been up and down this road so many times, it's all smooth now.'

'Just look at them,' said the owner of the premises, her voice betraying her feelings. 'They're a disgrace. Come on out, Nang 'Mai. It's you who's causing all the trouble. What is it you're all whispering about?'

'Mai, or Lamai, came out first, smiling, followed by Prasert, Chalaem, and Samorn, all of them beautifully dressed with their faces covered in powder. The room was filled with the scent of different perfumes. The more they looked at the young man, the more they all giggled. 'What's so funny about me, then?' Wit asked.

Among the beautiful girls crowding round him, however, there was one missing, and that was the one he was so desperate to see.

'Would you like to know something?' Lamai asked, leaning over towards him. She was quite good-looking. She was dressed all in red with a striking jacket of thin red silk with a plunging neckline that revealed her loose undergarment. 'You'll have to give me something if you do.'

'Ah, so Lamai's going to make a fool of me, then, is she, Chalaem?' said Wit, feigning innocence and grasping the upper arm of the girl sitting on the arm of his chair.

Chalaem smiled sweetly. 'Are you going to be our victim, then?' She had a rather plump figure and had clearly used a thick layer of powder to conceal the pallor of her face. Her hair was cut short in the style of the heroes of musical dramas.

Before Wit had a chance to reply, another girl thrust her head forward and said in mock-anger, 'If Khun Wit thinks we're making a fool of him, then we're not going to tell him what we're laughing about. Actually, though, he's really dying to know.'

'All right, I will,' said Wit decisively. 'Tell me how much you want each.'

'Oh, that's up to you. How can you expect us to make the rules? But Khun Wit's ever so kind,' Chalaem continued, flattering him, 'so he's bound to be generous.'

'Who says I'm kind? I shan't give you a thing,' he retorted defiantly. Outwardly he was joking and in high spirits; but inside he was restless and felt he was wasting his time playing about with these girls whom he had no wish to see. He stole frequent glances over in the direction of the doorway which was hidden behind the floral-patterned curtain.

Everyone began to protest so noisily that Samorn, who appeared to be older than the others, raised her hand for silence. 'All right, let's have a bit of quiet, then. How about this, then—we'll make a new deal with Khun Wit.'

'What kind of a deal?' the other girls cried out in unison.

'We'll make a deal that if Khun Wit likes what we say, then we get a reward,' she explained, eyeing Wit flirtatiously.

He was beginning to enjoy himself a little more. 'How

will you know whether or not I like what you say ?' he asked.

'Oh, that's as easy as anything. If you like it, you'll giggle,' she said with a challenging laugh. 'Is it a deal?'

'Hang on a minute. If I keep a straight face, it means you all lose, right? And then how much is each one of you going to give me?' Wit asked, looking round for Ba Taht. 'Hey, where's Ba Taht gone? I need a witness.'

'Well, we're all gamblers. If you win, we'll let you do what you like to us,' 'Sert announced loudly to her friends.

'You'll never do it,' said one of the girls. 'If you do, I'll let you clout me round the ear-holes an extra three times for luck.'

'Come on then, say it. Whoever's going to say it, come on and get it over with. And get ready for a clout round the ear-holes, too. This'll make a nice loud sound,' Wit added, as he grabbed one of the girls by the head and rubbed his hand hard against it.

'Listen, then,' said Lamai, who had started it all in the first place. 'I'll say it.' Her bright-red painted lips were close, almost touching Wit's cheek. 'We didn't want to come down and disturb you, Khun Wit, because we know that you don't want to see us. Khun Wit has come to see Reun, hasn't he?'

No sooner had she finished than there was the sound of laughter. 'Khun Wit loses, Khun Wit loses.'

Never had he thought that anything that those girls might say could give him such pleasure as to make him smile quite openly. 'All right, I lose. Anyone who wants it can go and get it from my jacket pocket over there.'

When he had finished, Prasert went and fetched him his wallet. He opened it and handed her a 5-baht note. 'Split it between you,' he said, and then, lowering his voice, he added, 'and please tell Reun to come down, too.'

Even as he spoke, the girl he wished to see was standing out of sight at the top of the stairs, reluctant to go down and see him. Her heart pounded as Wit's voice echoed up the stairs. Some powerful feeling held her back, a mere shadow at the top of the stairs. It was a feeling she herself still did not fully understand.

'Just a minute ago, she was on her way down,' said Samorn. 'I don't know why she went back up the minute she realized it was Wit. She keeps herself to herself these days and won't go with any customers. She just sits around looking miserable.'

'Who's that, then, Samorn?' asked Ba Taht, the owner of the premises, who had just come into the room and wondered what they were talking about.

'It's Reun, Ba. She's refused to go with anyone for several nights now. She keeps complaining of aches and pains.'

'What's the matter with her? Hasn't she come down, then?' Ba Taht looked round the room. 'Where's she gone and hidden herself? Every time I tell her that it's Khun Wit to see her, she looks as pleased as anything, you know. And Reun's certainly your favourite all right.' She grumbled on in her usual manner. But she dared not say too much about Reun because she knew that Reun was indeed Wit's favourite, and Wit was a young man with sufficient money to pay handsomely whenever he came to her establishment.

'She's a nice girl,' Ba Taht continued. 'The only thing wrong with her is that she's a bit unsophisticated, a bit of a country girl.'

'There's nothing wrong with being unsophisticated, Ba,' said Wit. 'I like people like that.'

'Ye-es.' Ba Taht's jaw dropped as she spoke. 'It's because you like her that Reun has started playing hard to get with the other customers. When anyone else comes, she doesn't want to see them.'

Wit laughed with delight. Ba Taht's account of Reun's behaviour had immediately changed the expression on his face. 'I'm not sure, perhaps she won't have me, either,' he said, without addressing anyone in particular.

'Well, if you want to know for sure, go upstairs and ask her for yourself. She's upstairs in her room. You know the way,' Ba Taht added, half seriously, half in jest. 'Ah, there we are. There's someone else banging at the gate now. 'Sert, go on, off you go and open up!'

Seizing the opportunity, Wit rose quickly from his chair and went through the adjoining room and up the stairs. At the top, he turned right until he came to a room which was closed but not locked. Slowly, he opened the door and stepped in. There, inside, a girl stood with her back to the door. She stood in silence among the dark shadows by the wall, her face buried in her hands. Wit moved close to her and put his arms around her, forcing her to turn round and face him. 'Reun,' he whispered, softly.

 Three

FROM behind, all he could see was her thick black hair, hanging down loose and uncombed, and her well-proportioned figure, clothed in a dark brown sarong and a plain white, short-sleeved blouse. Slowly, she turned from the dark shadows by the door and faced him, putting her hands up against his chest to stop him from pressing too closely against her. The face with which Wit had become infatuated was caught in the dim blue light. It was the face of a girl of about nineteen, gentle and honest, with a look of sadness about it. There was no trace of affectation or flirtatiousness about her, and she had none of the assured mannerisms and movements of Bangkok girls. Indeed, she was like a girl who had lived all her life far from the modern world and had only just, in the last few months, been introduced to it and instructed in its ways. She looked up and caught his gaze and then averted her eyes once more. They were moist with tears.

Wit took her two hands as they pressed against his chest and squeezed them gently. 'Reun, my darling, what's the matter?' he asked doubtfully. 'The moment you see me, you burst into tears. What are you crying for? Aren't you pleased to see me tonight?'

She looked up at him again. The tears that had been welling up in her eyes from the moment he saw her were now trickling down her cheeks, and the eyes which gazed at Wit were sad and heavy.

'Oh, Khun Wit,' Reun groaned. 'You shouldn't have saved such a question for now,' she continued in a trembling voice, scarcely more than a whisper. 'You should have asked me long ago, when you first met me.'

'I want to know your answer,' said Wit, leaning over to comfort her, 'about whether you're pleased I've come to see you. I haven't been for nearly a week. Didn't you miss me, my dear?'

'With you, I've never felt I had to force myself. If you wish me to answer, then I shall do so once more.' Her voice was soft and deep and prompted Wit to lean forward and kiss her gently on the forehead.

'At the moment I feel as if my heart is being split in two. One part of me feels happy and, more than anything else, wants you to be near. Even when you are gone for just two or three days, I feel sad and lonely, as if there's a vital part missing from my life. But for another part of me, it is such a torture to see you come here so often.'

'Is that really how you feel, Reun?' Wit asked quickly, looking deep into her eyes, as if searching for the truth.

'Yes,' the poor girl replied emphatically, 'that is the way I feel. If you weren't listening very carefully, you might not be very pleased to hear me say that seeing you is such torture. To tell you the truth, it's the exact opposite of the way I'd like things to be. The other girls would just think that seeing the man they loved and being close to him would make them happy. They wouldn't think of the damage that was being done to his honour and reputation.'

Wit drew in a deep breath. He was a strong and resolute man, in both mind and body; yet, before this loyal and honest girl, whom he had heard describing her love for him in such heart-rending terms, he became strangely weak.

'As for the likes of me, you know very well that I'm not beautiful, that I'm just a country girl in my manners, and that I'm not much good at anything or hardly anything. But even so, I really believe that I am different from other people in one way, and that is in my sincerity and desire for your well-being.'

'You don't have to tell me, Reun. I know very well how you feel about me. Don't cry now. Let's go and sit down over there. We shouldn't spend all our time standing up talking.'

Wit led her by the hand over to the bed on the left-hand side of the room. Reun tried to free her hand, but Wit held it tightly and would not let go, so she followed reluctantly. But in the end, an overwhelming power compelled her to sit down on the floor in front of the bed. She sat there with her face buried in Wit's lap and sobbed. Wit bent over her and tried to comfort her again. 'I love you,' he said, 'and you love me. Let's not think beyond that for the moment. How about looking up and giving me a smile? Give me a smile to show me you're pleased to see me.'

Like an obedient child, Reun looked up, her face bathed in tears, and smiled sadly at the man she loved even more than herself. But almost immediately, the smile disappeared.

'If I wasn't a prostitute living in this awful place, then I'd tell you this minute how terribly happy I was to see you. But it's not just out of selfishness that I love you. If a stupid girl like me has to go amusing herself in that kind of way, then I don't think that's love. It's just using people. Our positions and everything about us is different. You're from a wealthy and respectable family. You shouldn't be coming here to this... this brothel. I'm not even the kind of girl you should be mixing with. After all, I'm a prostitute.'

'Don't go blaming yourself like that, Reun. I, at least, know that you're good. You're not like the others.' Wit felt pity for her as he stroked her hair which lay in disarray across his lap.

'It's only you who think I'm not bad and that's because you know me. But what about other people? They're not as fair as you in what they think. They despise me and think I'm disgusting. They think that just coming near me will somehow damage or harm them,' Reun said, wiping her tears.

'Even if you think you're bad or others say you are, that's up to them. Whoever wanted to be a prostitute because they thought selling sex was fun and profitable? Just ask Samorn and Prasert. And even you, too, Reun. Do you like living here? Of course you don't. You all do it because you have to. Everyone has their own duties to perform. I have mine and you have yours. So who can say,' Wit added thoughtfully, 'who is good and who is bad? Come and sit here with me, Reun. I want to have a look at your face and see if you've stopped crying.'

Reun did as he asked and then buried her face against the young man's chest. 'Khun Wit, what you've said makes me feel a traitor to myself. I've been trying to warn you away from this evil, so I didn't want you to come here again. But you ... what am I supposed to say?'

'There's no need to say anything more, Reun,' said Wit, hugging the girl he really loved tightly. 'I understand everything you said. I keep on thinking that I must repay your sincere love.'

'Khun Wit,' Reun interrupted quietly, 'it's not in the hope of getting something in return that I love you. All I want you to know is that I, whom the world would condemn for feeling no real love and for selling sex for a living, love you. I really love you. That's all.'

'I know you love me. But we can't go on loving each other and carrying on like this. I intend to take you away from here to a place of our own, where you will have my name and be my wife.' The young man spoke sincerely, his voice full of optimism. 'If you continue to stay here, it will be difficult for you to stop me coming to see you again. The more I've got to know you, the more I've wanted to. And if I do something, it has to be because I want to, so when I decide to come and see you, it's because I want to.'

'But your father is a respectable *phaya*. Wouldn't you be ashamed to take a prostitute like me into your family?' Reun asked quietly. 'People would say things. Think about it carefully. Your brothers and sisters, at least. . . .'

Wit raised his hand before Reun could finish. 'I don't care what people say. It's our happiness. If it bothers us, we can go away, up-country. It'd be peaceful there, and there'd be no one to trouble us. But the main thing that worries me at the moment is that I have no income. All I've got at the moment is only a little—50 or 60 baht. It's true my father's rich. But if I decide to take you away from here, I don't want any of my family involved. They all despise anyone who's poor.'

'Goodness, you don't have to go to any trouble because of me,' Reun said unhappily. 'Just leave me here. I'm no better than any other prostitute. I shouldn't drag you away from your family.'

'I've just told you, I like doing what I like,' Wit said fiercely. In fact, deep down, he was still hurt by what his mother and other relatives had said. They had been unanimous and absolute in their refusal to allow him to bring into the house a girl whom they regarded as a wretched common prostitute.

'If I leave you here, I know you'll just become a plaything for other men. I can't do that. And another thing. A few minutes ago I heard the others say you hadn't been with another man for some time. Is that true?'

'Yes,' she replied. 'Ever since I thought I was really in love with you, I haven't wanted to let other men touch me.'

Wit did not put his thanks into words, but his eyes spoke louder than words as he gazed at the girl. 'The more I know about you, the more I feel concern for you. But while it's true that you and I are happy about that, Ba Taht won't be so pleased, because she's losing out a lot on you.'

'It's true what you say,' said Reun sadly. 'Ba Taht has been rather sarcastic to me.'

'And later she won't just be sarcastic. The reason she still treats you all right is because she's clever. She knows I love you, that I'm really fond of you, and that whenever I come, I give her money as a gesture of goodwill. If ever I were to have important business and couldn't come to see you often, she'd soon lose patience because she wouldn't be getting any money and that's when things would start getting difficult for you.'

The tears which had dried on Reun's face began to run again, but this time they were tears of happiness at what he had said. This was all she wanted from him. 'It doesn't matter,' she sobbed as she tried to compose herself. 'I've been used to hardship ever since I first came to live here. I've been beaten and cursed enough times to be used to it by now.'

'I know very well that you'd like to come and live with me, Reun, but you're worried that people will criticize and gossip, and my reputation will be ruined. Or if not that, you're afraid there will be other difficulties. I'm a man, Reun. Difficulties are nothing new to me.'

'You're still young, so you can afford to talk like that,' Reun warned. 'Later, in the future, if you think about it, you might be sorry that you took me as your wife. It wouldn't help you in getting on. It would just wreck things for you. You've always been surrounded by a circle of family, relatives, and friends. You've only ever known happiness. Do you think you could bear leaving all that for a life of hardship and suffering with me?'

'The more difficult things are, the harder I'll fight. Forget about those problems, Reun. It's simply a case of finding a job.'

'What kind of a job?' she asked briefly.

'Well, that's it. I'm in a bit of a fix there. It never ever occurred to me before to earn any money. All I've ever done is spend it. I've got to find some kind of work that'll bring in a little money each month, say 30 or 40 baht. That would enable us to have a little house of our own. There you are, then, Reun,' said Wit reassuringly, 'you feel a bit better now. And I'll try and hurry up and find a job to do for a bit. Maybe fate will make our dreams come true.'

'Even if you had a job and enough money to take me away, things wouldn't be quite as easy as that,' Reun murmured gloomily.

'Where do you see the problem, then?' Wit asked. 'You come and live with me and be my wife. That's settled. No problem. And we'll be happy, too, being together.'

'No problem,' said Reun, repeating Wit's words absent-mindedly. 'I don't deny that we'd be happy together in that little house you dream of. But such things aren't always possible.'

'Why not?' Wit interrupted.

'You're just like any other young man who loves a girl and dreams of perfect happiness with her. You can live anywhere, as long as it's with the girl you love, and you can overcome any obstacles in your way. This is only a passing feeling among men. But even if you are no different, please don't think that I'm criticizing you, or looking down on you for the love you feel towards me. That's the way you'll feel when it's all still new. You used to see your friends and go out with them, so you'd be bound to want to go out and enjoy yourself with them sometimes. True, you wouldn't have anything to do with your relatives or society, but you'd want to, at least, go and relax at the cinema. And if you loved your wife, you'd want to take her along, too. And if we went anywhere, like to the cinema, you might bump into some of your old friends, and how would you feel then, if you heard them whispering to each other, "That's Wit Adinan, the son of Phaya Aditepabodi, and that girl sitting there next to him is his wife. She used to live in Ba Taht's brothel. She's a prostitute."' Reun spoke softly in a shaky voice, her lips trembling with emotion.

'I don't give a damn about them, Reun,' said Wit defiantly. But he knew that what she had said was true.

'You may not take any notice of it at first, that's true. But if you keep on hearing it, it will begin to have an effect and it will make you unhappy. All you'll hear will be their gossip and spiteful remarks. No matter how much you love me, you won't be able to stand it. Just answer me honestly, now, Khun Wit, could you stand it? I'm serious.'

After considering in silence for a moment, Wit replied. 'Perhaps I could take it,' he said, half in resignation, half defiantly.

'And perhaps you couldn't,' Reun added. 'And then you'd ask yourself why you'd destroyed your reputation and why people no longer admired you as they used to. And eventually, wouldn't you come to realize that your fortunes had sunk so low because you'd married a prostitute, because you'd married me? But what about me? I, myself, couldn't stand it.

Not because of shame or embarrassment. Prostitutes like me are used to that. But if this were to happen to you, I myself just couldn't stand it. It's you I love more than anything. Do you think I could ever torture you indirectly in this way? I couldn't,' said Reun emphatically, 'I really couldn't.'

Wit allowed her to finish without interrupting, because when he heard what she had to say, his opposition and stubborn refusal to listen to other people's advice had gradually diminished, to the point where he felt almost totally discouraged. He managed to pull himself together and forced a smile.

'Well, that was a magnificent speech,' he said admiringly. 'I can scarcely believe you're a country girl who, as you said, has only been in Bangkok for six months. Where did you learn to speak like that?' he added jokingly.

Reun was not pleased by such words of praise from the man she loved and her face looked even sadder as she replied. 'Even if I am a country girl who's never had enough education, I know about these things because I've had some experience of them and because I've listened to people talking. Don't forget that here, in this—this brothel—there are other nice men, apart from you, who come frequently.'

'How do you know they're nice?' Wit asked.

'From what they say, from their manner, and from the way they behave. Important people you'd never have imagined have been here, too. I learn from these people. Some of them who know what life's all about offer me advice and teach me about life because they feel sorry for me and think I'm just a stupid country girl. But you, Wit, only you never despised me or looked down on me as a prostitute or thought of me as just a passing plaything. There are things about you that are different from other men. You understand me better than anyone. That's why I love you, love you without hoping for anything in return. I may be labelled a prostitute, but if it's

necessary, I can make any sacrifice for the honour and reputation of the one I love. My happiness and wishes don't come
into it.' Her determination showed in her eyes as she gazed
defiantly at the man she loved, until Wit had to look away.

'Come on, Reun, stop worrying about stupid old gossip.
Let's agree definitely, then, that it would be best to go and
live up-country. We'll go up north and get right away from
the kind of people who can't keep their mouths shut. We'll
grow rice and fruit and cultivate the land as man and wife.'

'You, cultivate the land!' Reun cried. But then fearing
Wit would think she was mocking him, she immediately
lowered her voice and spoke more softly. 'Darling, don't
think about living off the land when you don't even know
what a spade or a hoe looks like. I've used them. And I've
had enough experience of them to be able to tell you quite
simply that a hoe is bigger and heavier than the racquet that
you're used to. They're miles apart. Even real country people
themselves still find it hard and tiring. And you....' She left
her sentence unfinished, leaving him to draw his own conclusion.

'Let's stop talking and thinking about this now, Reun. I
came here to make you happy, to try to cheer you up, and to
encourage us to fight and overcome all obstacles. Remember?'

Reun shook her head hopelessly and buried it in Wit's lap
once more. The sound of conversation gradually faded until
it was lost completely in the sound of rain which had been
falling steadily since dusk. From time to time, other sounds
could be heard, sounds which one should not dwell on when
there are so many other more interesting things.

Four

CONTINUOUS rain throughout the previous night had left the early morning air rather cool. Reun awoke with a start. Lying close against Wit's warm body, she still felt drowsy, but anxiety and concern forced her to slowly extricate herself from his embrace. In the first place, what made her feel sad and unable to go back to sleep was that it was almost daylight, and Wit would have to leave. She propped herself up on one elbow and looked closely at the face of the man she loved as he lay there asleep. The forehead, the eyebrows, the tightly closed eyelids, the nose, the mouth, even his skin—they all clearly announced that he was from a high-class family. Yet, this man was really hers.

'If I were like some girls who think only of themselves, you would have to belong to me. Wit, my darling, I'm labelled a worthless, despicable girl. It would be difficult to keep you all to myself. Your worth and reputation are more important than my wishes. Even if I were just an ordinary girl, and not a prostitute who has sunk to such depths, wouldn't you still belong to someone else? For you to be mine,' she moaned sadly, 'I would have to fight, fight to the last breath of my life.' She fought back her sobs with difficulty when she heard the Indian night watchman in the distance beating his metal gong five times. She leaned over and whispered softly in Wit's ear as he lay there fast asleep.

'Khun Wit!'

'Hmmm?' he murmured and moved slightly. Then he yawned and curled up again under the warm blanket. She felt sorry for him; he was really sleeping so peacefully. Reun thought back to what Wit had said about them living to-gether in a little house. He looked so contented like this, she wouldn't try to disturb him again. She'd let him sleep until it was light, until late in the morning. No, no, she couldn't do that. She leaned over him and tapped him gently on the arm.

'Khun Wit! Khun Wit!'

'Mmmm?' There was another murmur and he turned over towards Reun. Somewhat reluctantly, Wit opened his sleepy eyes. He brushed Reun's head fondly with one hand and was about to close his eyes again, when Reun said, 'Wake up, it's almost daylight.'

'What do you mean, "daylight"? It's still dark,' Wit grumbled drowsily. 'You're having me on.'

'Khun Wit, it's almost daylight, really,' Reun persisted.

'And to hell with it if it is. What's up? Are you trying to get rid of me?' he continued, grumbling. Then realizing his last sentence might offend Reun, he quickly changed his tone. 'Let me have just a little bit longer, my darling,' he pleaded. 'I just want to lie close to you.'

'Oh, you are awful,' Reun sighed as if she was offended. She watched in silence as he closed his eyes for a moment and looked as if he was going to start snoring again. This time she certainly wasn't going to let him. She reached over and gave him a shake.

'Khun Wit, open your eyes a moment. Darling, I've got something to tell you.'

'Darling, can't it wait until daylight?' he asked without opening his eyes. 'I'm sleepy and it's so comfortable here. Why did you wake up when it's still so dark? Come on back to bed, Reun.'

'Khun Wit, I want you to go home before it's daylight. Can you hear what I'm saying?' she said, speaking right into his ear.

Eyes now wide open, Wit looked doubtful. 'Yes, but why, Reun?'

'It's best to go while it's still dark. If you wait until day-light, people will see you.'

Wit laughed softly. 'Oh damn them. Let them think what they like. I'm not a burglar sneaking back home, you know.'

Reun heaved a deep sigh of frustration. 'That's not it at all. I'm worried that if anyone sees you around the town at such an early hour, it will be harmful for your reputation.'

'I'm a man,' Wit countered, with a yawn.

'Believe me, please. Get up and have a wash and then get dressed and go home. I don't want you to go at all, but you understand my reasons perfectly well. You don't know how hurtful gossip can be. At the very least, it can upset you for a long time. Get up, now, please,' she said, cajoling and pleading with him.

Wit tried to put her off three or four times. It was beginning to get warmer. And really, he couldn't ignore Reun's advice which was sensible. He got up from the bed, and even before he had finished dressing, day began to dawn.

Reun followed him downstairs to see him off. She put his raincoat over his arm and handed him his grey woollen hat. Her eyes came to rest sadly on Wit. He felt pity for her and squeezed her hands to comfort her.

'Being forced out of bed in this manner only makes me more determined. I'll try everything I can to get a job, Reun. Wish us luck. So we won't have to part the way we do today.'

Tears began to trickle down Reun's cheeks when she heard these words, clearly, with her own ears. She flung herself into Wit's arms and buried her face in his chest, and although her tears were still fresh, she looked up at him and laughed. As she did so, she pushed him away from her and said brusquely, 'Go on. Off you go, now.'

Wit felt heavy-hearted as he looked closely at Reun. She presented an unhappy sight that filled him with pity. He stood, silently enrapt, as he gazed at the forlorn figure leaning against the doorway in front of him. This was the girl who had made his mother faint on the spot at the mere mention that he was going to live with her; this was the girl over whom his elder sister had refused him any assistance when he wanted to bring her home; this was the girl whom everyone looked down on and condemned as a prostitute; and yet— this was the girl who had only his best interests at heart.

He pulled her close to him again and stroked her arms. 'I'll be off now, Reun, but I'll come again in a couple of days.' He did not dare look at her face which was bathed in tears. He turned away but he had hardly taken three steps when he suddenly remembered something and stopped. He dug his hand into his shirt pocket and walked back. 'Here, Reun, take this. Give some to Ba Taht. Otherwise she might insist on you doing something you don't want to.'

She held out her hand and took the bundle of folded notes, without unfolding and counting them. Her sad black eyes shone with gratitude. 'Think of me sometimes,' she whispered, unable to stop herself.

'You need have no worries about that, because we're almost one and the same person now. So cheer up a bit. But let me just warn you about one little thing. Ba Taht isn't very pleased about you not going with other customers. We still have no choice but for you to keep in with her and not let her get annoyed with you. To people like her, money is more important than anything. By that, I really don't mean to look down on her. Money certainly is more desirable than other things. I told her that I would be happy to.... I think you know what I mean.' He left the last sentence unfinished for Reun to interpret what he meant. He squeezed her cold hand again before turning and walking out of the gate.

The sound of the gate slamming shut made her feel, as she stood watching him disappear from sight, that her whole life and soul had also suddenly departed with him. She stood there in a daze for a while and then, suppressing her feelings, went back up to her bedroom. She lay down and stretched out on the same spot where Wit had slept. The scent of his hair was still fresh on her pillow. She lay there in silence, trying to fill her mind with pleasant memories rather than thoughts of her troubles. He had told her that he would take her away from here to a small house, far away from his family and friends, far away from society. Reun did not dare to hope for too much, except in her dreams, because she was only too well aware that she was no better than a prostitute.

More than anything else, Reun dreamed of a small house, set in a quiet and peaceful place, far away from people. She had once seen a house in Bangseu which she really liked. It was a single-storey house on stilts, with three rooms and a concrete floor underneath. On the outside, it was painted pale blue and on the inside, a cream colour. On the ground, set apart from the house, was a kitchen and bathroom, while around the house, there were various kinds of fruit-trees, such as mangoes, longans, and rose-apples. Reun dreamed that her house would be just like that one, although it was hardly something that she could be very certain about. She would not let herself get carried away with dreams of anything too wonderful, because if Wit could not find a well-paid job, she might have to live in some tiny house or shack. But that would be nothing new. All she wanted was happiness and the freedom to arrange things as she pleased, and finally, to have Wit. What was the use of having a huge, beautiful house? Reun allowed her thoughts to wander freely to provide some respite from her unhappiness. Her eyes gazed out of the wide-open window until they gradually became heavier and finally closed completely out of exhaustion.

*   *   *

Who would have thought that this face and this small body lying here, exhausted, had, six or seven months earlier, belonged to a carefree, innocent, and untainted young village girl? Everyone in Thepharat District of Chachoengsao Province, whatever their age, could still remember Wahn, the daughter of Ta Kert and Yai Im, for Wahn was as sweet and as gentle as her name suggested and was loved by everyone. Yet she had left them and the district in a way that none of them would have dreamed possible.

Long after it was known all over the district that Wahn had left, people would still say, 'My goodness, on Songkran Day, she went to make merit at this very temple, and I actually said to her, "My goodness, you're all dressed up today." You wouldn't think it was possible, would you? It's Ta Kert and Yai Im I feel sorry for. They've only got the one daughter, although there are the boys, Wong and Wing, of course. If Wahn was still here, they would have had her to look after them.' Those who had daughters and granddaughters warned them not to be like Wahn and told them they should love their parents and brothers and sisters. Some said she was just a worthless slut.

However, it was indeed just as people said. On Songkran Day, Wahn had gone with her parents and two brothers to offer food to the monks at the temple. She had been happy and excited. The merit-making ceremony at the temple was a public festival, an occasion for getting dressed up and showing off new clothes and a chance for people in the district to get to see each other. It was an opportunity Wahn was not going to miss. She woke early that morning and collected together various savouries and sweetmeats to put in the boat. Then she paddled her way over to the temple, where she went and joined all the other villagers listening to the monks praying in the pavilion. As she sat there, her eyes shifted from face to face, as she looked for people she knew and tried to see if this girl or that girl was there or not. As she looked around, another pair of eyes, staring straight at her, met her gaze. She felt embarrassed and averted her eyes, but she could not help stealing a furtive glance when the opportunity arose. Those bright, piercing eyes belonged to an elegant-looking young man. Extremely slim and rather delicate in appearance, he was wearing a patterned blue silk shirt and trousers of the same colour, while on his wrist, there was a gold watch. He was not from this district, which meant that he could only be from Bangkok.

From Bangkok. The mere thought made her heart pound with excitement. She could see that both his manner and style of dress were different from the young men chatting loudly at the jetty. Wahn knew several of them. One of them was Feun, Ta Saeng's son. Behind him was Perm, the son of their neighbour, Lung Sorn, and then there were Uam, Kaeo, and several others. They seemed to be having a good time, pointing out the girls to each other and laughing. While they didn't exactly look like buffaloes, they were not much better than cattle. They seemed so ordinary to her. But this newcomer, thought Wahn, he was attractive. When he smiled, you could see the gold tooth which was normally concealed in the corner of his mouth. And she wasn't the only one who had noticed him, either, for several other girls were also casting glances in his direction.

When the monks began to chant, people crowded forward to grab a bowl so that they could make food offerings outside the temple pavilion. Temple boys brought the monks' alms bowls forward and arranged them in a row on a bench that had been set up outside, with the lids placed by the side of the bowls. The sound of people shouting and calling out to each other mingled with the monks' chanting. Men and women, young and old alike, were crushed against one another in the rush, as they struggled to serve out rice from the dishes they were holding into the monks' alms bowls. There was an endless sea of hands moving back and forth.

Yai Im pushed someone aside and handed a bowl of rice to her daughter, who was standing a little apart from the crowd.

'Here, Wahn, go and put this in, quickly. Push your way in, in front of Maen. Go on.'

Wahn took the dish from her mother and, going right to the front of the row, she squeezed herself in on the left of the girl called Maen. With her head and eyes lowered, she served a little rice into each of the alms bowls until she reached the middle of the row. At that moment, she felt somebody bump into her from behind. She was annoyed and turned round sharply to see who it was. Her expression changed instantly to one of shyness and she quickly looked away. Who else could it have been, but the man with the piercing eyes? He stared at her with undisguised surprise. Later, when she thought about this, she felt her heart pounding. Why this should have been so, even she herself could not really say.

Wahn did not see the man again until the merit-making ceremony was over and she was about to get into the boat to go home. She was just taking the food trays down to the boat which was secured in front of the banyan tree dam, when, lo and behold, there he was, sitting next to Feun in a dug-out boat moored next to hers. She pretended not to notice and turned back to her mother to take the things as they were handed down to her. Just then, she heard Feun calling.

'Hey, Wahn! Wahn!'

She turned round, her face expressionless. But inside she felt embarrassed when she saw him staring at her with a broad grin on his face. 'What did you call me for?' she asked.

'We're going back now and Perm's getting up a game of cards. We're short, so how about joining us?' Feun suggested. 'And your mother, too. Will you come and play, too?' he asked, extending the invitation to Yai Im.

Yai Im made an excuse. 'My eyes and ears aren't so good. She'll go, though.'

Wahn feigned reluctance. 'They've already invited me over to Lung Ngiam's.'

'Well, it won't be much fun at Ngiam's house,' said Feun, 'playing with silly old folk. Come over to Perm's house. It'll be much better, and it's near your house, too. How about it?'

Before she had time to reply, Perm interrupted. 'Come on, Wahn. Come and help us do this Bangkok fellow.' At this, all the young men burst out laughing.

Wahn's face went numb when she heard them say 'do this Bangkok fellow'. He really was from Bangkok, then, as she'd guessed, and he must be going to play cards at Perm's house as well. She hesitated for a moment before agreeing, and then, with her eyes lowered, she pushed off from the bank with her paddle. All the way back, the young man's face kept floating round and round in the back of her mind. She was so lost in her own thoughts that it startled her when she heard her mother say to her father, 'Who on earth's that young man, then?'

'Which one?' he asked doubtfully, looking up while continuing to roll his nipa leaf cigarette.

'That one in Feun's boat, of course. The one in the silk trousers. . . .'

'Ah,' he said before she could finish, almost causing Wahn to stop paddling as she waited for what would come next. 'I don't know him,' he continued. 'Looks as if he is from Bangkok. Funny-looking fellow. Looks like a real womanizer.'

A look of disapproval unconsciously flashed across Wahn's face when she heard her father describe the young man as a womanizer without ever having met him, even once. Her father was always criticizing people. Anyone would agree that he was ten times better than her brothers, Wong and Wing. Her thoughts were in turmoil all the way home. When she had put away the dishes and things they had used at the merit-making ceremony, she bathed quickly and dressed herself up in her best clothes. She took along with her the money she had earned from picking up the fallen rice ears during the threshing season, and went straight off to Perm's house. Her heart was already there. Within this beautiful, innocent girl, a strange new feeling had been born, a feeling which, as it secretly and gradually emerged, filled her with happiness.

Five

WHEN Wahn arrived at Lung Sorn's house, everyone was already seated on reed mats. It looked as if they were all waiting, for her. She caught sight of his face immediately, before she noticed any of the others. Apart from him, Perm, Lung Sorn's son, Feun, Bunreuan, Tiap, and several other people she knew well were all there. Wahn congratulated herself for appearing calm and composed, but inside, her heart was beating unusually fast.

'Ah, so you've arrived at last,' Perm greeted her. 'Everyone's been waiting for you. We almost had to send Poom off to get you. Sit down. Over there. They've saved a place for you.'

Wahn was startled. Where Perm had told her to sit was right next to the man from Bangkok. Who could have sat down under the circumstances? She was unable to maintain her composure any longer. 'Oh no,' she said. 'Let me sit next to Reuan.'

'Hey,' cried Feun, 'where am I supposed to sit, then? It's all right the way they've arranged it, with boys and girls sitting alternately. You've got the Bangkok fellow to worry about,' he added, and everyone laughed.

The man from Bangkok spoke for the first time. 'You don't have to worry about me,' he said. 'I'm a hopeless player.' He was gentle, both in his speech and appearance, and so completely different from the young men of the village, whom she'd only ever heard shouting loudly and speaking coarsely. He sounded so pleasant that, not wishing to appear reluctant, she went and sat down shyly next to him.

At first, Wahn did not win a single hand, because she was not interested in either the cards she was holding or those which the others played. Her mind was too preoccupied with the person on her right. Feun had addressed him as 'Khun Wichai'. Wichai was a name she had never come across before in her life. All she had ever heard were names like Feun and Perm. The most unusual and the nicest-sounding name in the district belonged to Kamnan Sai's son, who was called 'Prasit'. But Wahn had never heard anyone call him by his full name. He was simply called 'Sit' or 'Ai Sit' by those who knew him well. But Feun had honoured this Bangkok fellow by calling him 'Khun Wichai'. There was no doubt he was well-off, and he was bound to be from a very respectable family. Wahn remembered that in the morning he had been wearing light blue, but now, he was sitting here in green silk trousers and a white silk vest. When he threw down a card in her direction, the large diamond ring on his index finger sparkled. More and more, Wahn felt that she would like to know exactly who he was and something about his personal life. Her curiosity was soon satisfied, for after another moment's play, she heard Perm say, 'I'm really sorry you've got to go back in five days' time, Khun Wichai. If you didn't, I'd take you to see some pretty girls.'

'I don't want to go back yet, either, Perm,' Khun Wichai replied, 'but I'm only on leave. Being a government official now isn't like it used to be in the old days. The salary is low and the workload heavy. Besides, I don't want to bother Pu Yai Nuam by staying too long.'

Wahn remembered everything he said. He was a govern-ment official—someone important even though he was still young. He was on leave now and staying at the home of the village headman, Nuam.

'Forgive me, sir, but how much do you earn?' Lung Sorn called from the back, asking what everyone wanted to know.

'Oh, not very much, Lung. Just over a hundred a month.'

Good Lord! Almost everyone there, Wahn included, was amazed. Over a hundred a month and still he called it, 'not very much'. In this part of the country, incomes were calcu-lated by the year and they got only 80 baht a year. If that was how much government officials earned, it was hardly surpris-ing that Khun Wichai was so smartly dressed and wore a large diamond ring and a gold wrist-watch.

'Oooh!' exclaimed Bunreuan. 'Do you get through all of it, the whole hundred?'

Khun Wichai was amused. 'How could it be enough?' he laughed. 'I have to go troubling my parents every month for several hundred.'

'Heavens!' cried Perm loudly. 'Hey, Tiap, what have you suddenly woken up for? And you've got your eyes wide open now, have you, Porng?' He played his turn but he was still curious. 'Don't your parents mind how you spend it?' he asked, staring across the circle.

'Don't be stupid,' said Feun. 'Khun Wichai's father is a *khun phra*. He owns lots of rice mills and sawmills. And did you know that the theatre troupe which is performing over at Khlong Suan belongs to Khun Wichai himself?'

'Oooh,' cried several voices in unison. But not Wahn's. She remained as composed as before. Khlong Suan was the name of a district which was the trading centre serving Thepharat. There was a theatre there and a market which served as a meeting place. She had heard from her girlfriends that a musical drama troupe from Bangkok had come out to play there. But she had no idea that the troupe belonged to Khun Wichai. To Khun Wichai, who was the son of a *khun phra* who owned lots of sawmills and rice mills.

'My father sometimes gets angry with me for being extravagant with money. But despite the way he goes on, he's really kind underneath. One moment he'll be cursing me and then the next, he's handing me two or three hundred,' said Wichai casually, as if 200 or 300 baht were the same as 2 or 3 baht. This made the group of card players even more astonished.

'Actually, he has no idea I'm here. I sneaked off and followed the theatre troupe. I was getting so depressed at home. My father is trying to force me to marry the daughter of a Chinese millionaire but my mother won't agree. She wants to marry me off to the daughter of a *phaya*. I was getting so fed up I decided to clear off for good. Hang on a minute there, Wahn. What was that you just put down? I didn't see.'

She had not been expecting him to turn and ask her something while she was off guard. 'A four,' she mumbled, not daring to add the polite word *ka* because she had never used it before while to use *ja* would have sounded funny. He was the son of a *khun phra*, she thought, sighing inwardly. He was destined for the daughter of a Chinese millionaire or the daughter of a *chao phraya*. And what about her? Better not to think about it. She forced herself to concentrate on the game of cards. She had been almost cleaned out without realizing it. Hey! That was a funny thing for Wichai to do. She had just seen him pick up the queen and here he was throwing it down again. This time Wahn won. Then she won again. And again. And again, until the money piled up in front of her lap was several times the amount she had brought with her from home. While everyone suspected why Wahn was the only person winning, no one dared to call out loud, 'Give me a chance too, Khun Wichai.' Wahn sat there calmly, winning until they stopped playing. Tiap complained that she had lost a whole 5 baht. Feun had lost 3 and Bunreuan and Perm had each lost more than 1 baht. Wahn smiled with satisfaction: she had won more than 10 baht. Only Khun Wichai laughed as if it did not bother him one little bit. He opened up his wallet and took out several 10-baht notes. He lay them down and then, glancing up, said he had brought 50 baht with him and now had only 35 left.

There was no mistaking that as they returned home after playing cards, everyone's curiosity in the young man from Bangkok had been fuelled. Among the card players, Wahn had some peculiar thoughts of her own. Why had he let her win? Did he have some special feelings for her? It was a waste of time to even think about it. Who was going to take any notice of her, a mere farmer's daughter? Even the daughters of a *chao phraya* and a Chinese millionaire were not good enough for him.

That evening Wahn looked at herself in the mirror many times. She ran a large comb through the thick, jet-black folds of her slightly wavy hair. Fortunately, unlike many country girls, she did not chew betel. She tried out a smile, showing her small teeth. She felt that she was every bit as good-looking as some of the Bangkok girls she had seen in Thepharat. 'Once someone told me what lovely eyes I had,' Wahn murmured to herself, 'and they said I was as sweet as you would expect with my name,' she added, rambling on in the foolish, dreamy manner of young girls of eighteen or nineteen.

Later in the evening, several of her girlfriends came over by boat to collect her for a game of *mae sri kao pii ling* over at the rice-threshing platform at Yai Chaeng's house, which was the biggest in the village. Wahn saw several young men gathered there, waiting for the girls. Everyone was in high spirits and having a good time.

Three or four hurricane lamps had been hauled to the top of some of the poles by pulleys and the lights from these lamps shone on the pale powdered faces of the girls as they sat in a large circle round the outside, smiling happily as they watched the game. People were trying to persuade Wahn to be *mae sri*. She always agreed, every year, because they said she was more beautiful than anyone else. The young men in the village would be jealous enough to even come to blows because of the lovely *mae sri*. But on this occasion, despite their pleas, she refused. Wahn had suddenly become shy, something she had never felt before. Who could take the part? Look, there was Khun Wichai, standing next to Pu Yai Nuam's son, watching. Why did he keep following her and staring at her all the time? she wondered. Each time their eyes met, Wahn looked away, feeling embarrassed.

As she sat there, singing the chorus part with the other girls, Wahn noticed that several of them, such as Ob and Term, were whispering among themselves and also taking a good look at her young Bangkok man. Some were calling out to attract his attention and Wahn could not help feeling jealous when Khun Wichai turned around. Why this was the case she could not tell.

Then Nai Am, a stocky-looking fellow, volunteered to be the monkey. Wahn did not take much interest in the *kao pii* part of the game. She just sat there quietly, allowing her thoughts to wonder until she heard a loud commotion, and the sound of old women and children fleeing in confusion, bumping into one another as they ran. It was certainly fun, but scary too. The monkey spirit now possessed Am. Wahn thought it was funny but a bit frightening. Am was ambling along like a gorilla, baring his white teeth as he chased first one person, and then another. Wherever he went, everyone would scatter, shrieking. 'Want some shrimp paste, ape-man?'

some of the young men mocked as they stood poking their faces at him. The 'monkey' Am growled and tried to grab them. They tried to make him chase them and purposely provoked him to anger so that he would roar like a real monkey. But he was a strange monkey ... a monkey that liked to run the same way the girls went. Wahn's thoughts were interrupted as 'monkey' Am ran straight towards where she and her girlfriends were standing. Startled, they all screamed amid the sound of laughter and young men shouting. Trembling, Wahn ran out ahead, but the monkey continued to follow behind. With a single leap, as if jumping across a ditch, she broke away from the rest of the girls and rushed behind a haystack.

Immediately, she crashed into someone else who had come to hide there. She staggered and fell on her backside and could not get up. She felt suddenly cold all over when that person bent down as if to embrace her. He touched her. He grabbed her arm and whispered in her ear, 'Wahn, I love you.'

Wahn was overcome with shock, excitement, and happiness. She had actually heard it with her own ears. It was not a dream. She was not imagining it. Khun Wichai sat down beside her in the dark shadow of the pile of straw. 'I love you,' he repeated.

No man had ever touched her or whispered things like this to her before. Wahn sat numb with shock. She heard all his sweet words. It felt nice when he touched and caressed her. Why then didn't she say something? She meant to tell him not to fall in love with her because she was a country girl, but she was too dazed. Then she heard the voices of the other girls calling her and, feeling embarrassed, she pulled herself together. She pushed Khun Wichai away and tried to get up. But he grabbed her hand and pulled her back.

'First tell me you love me,' he pleaded. 'Then I'll let you go.'

'Khun Wichai! Let me go. I ... can't love you. You're from Bangkok and I'm just a country girl,' Wahn replied hesitantly. The sound of the other girls calling came nearer. If anyone saw her alone with Khun Wichai in the dark, there was no doubt they would spread it all round the village. 'Goodness, they're coming. Come on. Let go of me!'

'First say you love me and then tomorrow night meet me at the haystack behind Lung Sorn's house,' said Wichai, almost as if he were issuing an order. For some reason, she nodded wearily in agreement. He immediately released her and she rushed out to see her friends, her mind in utter turmoil.

No one suspected anything. However, Wahn was uneasy all the way home. All night long, she lay awake thinking. She felt elated. She woke early and wished night would come quickly. When darkness fell, she slipped away to meet him as arranged. In the end, Wahn began to fancy that she really did love him. But what she thought was love was sexual desire, so she willingly gave herself to the man she loved.

Every night after that, Wahn slipped away to meet Khun Wichai. She listened to his passionate words of love and to his stories about the beauties and luxuries, the fun and pleasures of Bangkok. There, there were beautiful silk clothes of every kind and every colour. Whatever you wanted—as long as it was not the moon and stars—you could get there.

When Wichai saw that Wahn had grown to trust him, he invited her to go and live with him in Bangkok. After he had pleaded with her for a while, there was no longer any doubt as to whether or not she would agree. The idea of going to Bangkok had already appealed to her. She had seen Bangkok girls who had been out here. They wore lovely clothes and they looked really attractive. The way they walked and sat was different from the villagers. Wahn yearned to be like them. Her love and concern for her parents slowed down her preparations but only a little. Once she had made up her mind to go to Bangkok, she mentioned to Wichai that she had a few pieces of gold jewellery, such as a belt, a necklace, a string of beads, and a ruby ring. Wahn had not planned on taking those things with her because her parents were old now and were not able to work as easily as before, especially if they no longer had the daughter who was the main source of labour for rice farming. They would be poorer than before, but they could have her jewellery as a safeguard against poverty. Wichai, however, was opposed to the idea.

'I don't want to ask you to take a single thing with you. I'd like you to just take yourself. There's no need to bring clothes. There are plenty in Bangkok and you can have what you want. I've got enough money to buy them for you.' He paused for a moment before continuing. 'But you see, Wahn, just think for a minute. If you don't take any of them with you, what are people going to think when they see you? They might start gossiping that my wife hasn't got any jewellery. Isn't that a fact, what I'm saying?'

Why should it not be a fact? Indeed, it was this very fact which led Wahn to secretly take her mother's large 2-baht gold bracelet and add it to her own things. All of these items of jewellery had been earned by toiling away in the fields, but the bracelet, so Wahn had heard her mother say, was an old one inherited from Wahn's grandparents. Wahn persuaded herself that if things worked out, she would come back to see her mother with some money.

That night Wichai paddled up to the jetty to pick Wahn up. She carried her rattan bag down into the boat, tears streaming down her face. Her parents and brothers were still fast asleep in the house. The next morning there would be a big commotion when they discovered that she had disappeared with the man from Bangkok. Her parents would have no daughter to get food for them. Her brothers Wong and

Wing would have no one to tease and help them with planting and harvesting the rice. She sat crying throughout the journey while Wichai tried to comfort her sympathetically.

The next morning, he led her on board the Bangkok-bound boat. With an unhappy look on his face, he told Wahn, as they sat together on the boat, that he did not yet dare to take her straight to his parents' house that day, because if he took her home without prior warning, his parents would not have time to prepare themselves to meet his wife and get the house ready. He would take her to stay in a hotel first. Wahn had never heard the word 'hotel' before and did not know what it was. Her anxieties about where they were going to stay eased when Wichai explained that a hotel was a large beautiful building with lots of rooms, and that each room had a bed and mosquito net, as well as a desk and chair. He went on to say that food was provided, that people staying there paid 3 or 4 baht a day, rather like rent, and that they would only stay there for a day.

As they drove from the jetty, Wahn was overwhelmed with excitement at seeing so many beautiful houses and huge buildings. She did not note, or if she did, she could not have been able to remember the way the car was going. All she knew was that the streets were full of people milling around. She had not got over her initial excitement when the car entered a small lane and parked in front of the steps of a building. Wahn carried her bag out and followed Wichai up to the top floor of the building, bewildered and nervous. A neatly dressed old Chinese man came out to receive them. Wahn felt uneasy when she saw the strange way the Chinese man looked at her. Wichai exchanged a few words with him and he turned and shouted to a Chinese boy to take them to the end room. This, then, Wahn gradually realized, was what they called a hotel. There were lots of rooms arranged in a row. The room where she and Wichai were to stay was spacious with a double bed, a mosquito net and blankets, and even a bathroom. Wahn had never seen anything like it in all her life. Bangkok really had such fine things.

That evening, after ordering fish and rice to eat in their room, Khun Wichai dressed to go out, saying that he was going round to tell his parents about her. He did not return until dusk. As soon as Wahn saw his face, her heart began to pound because he wore an unhappy expression.

'My parents are furious with me,' he began ominously, 'so much so that they have cut me off and won't let me even step foot in the house. They cursed me for not liking the girl they had found for me. But don't worry. We'll go and stay with my aunt for a couple of days and wait for my parents to get over it. Then we'll try again.' He spoke in a way which led her to think that he really loved her; besides, wasn't his rejection of the girl his parents had found for him evidence of this?

So the following morning, Wahn left the hotel with Khun Wichai for his aunt's house. All the way, she was beset by little niggling doubts. Having always lived at home with her parents, she was beginning to realize that living with some-one else was not going to be as nice as she had originally anticipated. Even though she consoled herself that Wichai would be with her, deep down she had a strange sense of unease which she could not quite put into words.

Khun Wichai's aunt's house, which Wahn later learned was in Phraeng Sanphasat, was a two-storey building with a small pale blue wooden fence. As soon as she stepped into the house, the first thing that caught her eye was the sight of three or four girls sitting crowded round a sweetmeat vendor in front of the steps. They were all dressed in gaudy colours and had pale faces. When she realized she had become the object of their stares, Wahn avoided their eyes and turned away in embarrassment, without noticing the peculiar way they were all staring at her. All she heard was Khun Wichai greeting them warmly, using words she did not understand. They must be the daughters or nieces of his aunt, thought Wahn as she determinedly quickened her step and followed Khun Wichai into a room. Once she had sat down, Wichai told her to greet his aunt who was sitting on a mat in the middle of the room.

Slowly, she looked up and raised her hands, palms together, in front of her chest. Her eyes fell on Wichai's aunt's face. In an instant, she abandoned all her efforts to keep her spirits up. Her heart sank. She had never before in her life been afraid of any woman. Yet Wahn felt apprehensive and out of tune with Wichai's aunt from the very moment she set eyes on her.

Six

HER sharp features concealed the cunning in her cruel, hard eyes wherein lay a degree of ruthlessness. A lump of chewing tobacco lodged in her lower gum made her lips protrude. Her short neck matched her fat, shapeless body, while her clothes gave no clue to her wealth. As she greeted them with a laugh, her voice sent a shudder of fear through the country girl sitting opposite her.

'Well, well, well! And what has my nephew been up to all this time? You never come and see your aunt these days. How are your mother and father? And who's this, here, then? She looks a nice girl.'

'I've been up-country for a couple of weeks,' Wichai replied, 'that's why I haven't been round to see you for some time. This is Wahn, my wife. It's because of my parents that I've got to come troubling you, Aunt, and asking for your help.'

'Oh, I see,' his aunt said wearily. 'Well, what's it all about this time, then?'

'It's about me bringing Wahn back with me. They're absolutely furious. They accuse me of being ungrateful, because I don't like the rich girl they've found for me. They've barred me from the house, and now, they've cut me off and said they wouldn't even have me at their funerals. I tried to plead with them. I pointed out that Wahn wasn't as poor as they thought, that she was actually the daughter of a wealthy man, and that she loved me very much and wanted to be with me. But they wouldn't believe me. See for yourself, Aunt,' Wichai said, nodding in the direction of Wahn. 'There she is, all dressed up like this and still they say she's poor.'

His aunt cast a sharp eye in the direction indicated by Wichai. Wahn just sat still, her head bowed and her face flushed as she tried to hide the shame she felt when she heard him describing her as the daughter of a wealthy man. A wealthy man who had to sow his own rice, and who had a tiny hut and a couple of buffaloes to plough the paddy fields? She felt ashamed. What she was wearing was not the result of being wealthy, but the result of her own toil and sweat, of hours spent picking up the fallen ears of rice in the harvesting season and making sweets which she peddled along the canals. Wichai had gone too far in his compliments. He should have just said that his wife was not poor. That would have been quite enough.

'How could your parents do such a thing? Especially when their daughter-in-law looks like this. The moment they see her,' Wichai's aunt continued, 'their anger will all melt away.'

'I daren't take her to meet them. Please, Aunt, can Wahn and I stay with you for two or three days to give me a chance to sort things out with my parents?' His tone sounded rather impatient quite different from what one would expect if he was speaking to an older relative.

'That's all right. I'm only worried that Wahn might object, though. The house is rather small,' his aunt added, addressing Wahn for the first time, 'and I've got lots of daughters and nieces.'

Wahn felt confused, but before she had time to reply, Wichai interrupted on her behalf. 'Of course she doesn't mind. You can put up with anything as long as you're happy, can't you, Wahn?' He laughed and she forced a little smile, although she still felt afraid.

After that, Wichai's aunt called several of her daughters, including Win and Prasert, to go and prepare a room upstairs. For a short time, the sound of things being moved about above and the intermittent laughter of girls could be heard. Then a girl in a red skirt and low-neck blouse came running down the stairs and told Wichai, who was busy reassuring Wahn that, underneath, his aunt really had a heart of gold, that the room was now ready for them. Despite the girl's provocative attire, Wahn could sense friendship in her eyes, and a feeling of sympathy or even some strange kind of pity. She brushed the incident aside then but it occurred to her later that the look in Samorn's eyes on the first day of her arrival was one of profound sadness, like the look in a prisoner's eyes when he watches a new inmate arrive at the cells.

Wichai's aunt stood with her hands on her hips in the room that had been prepared for Wahn and him. She glanced up as she saw the two of them come in and gave them a welcoming smile. 'I do hope you don't mind the room being so small and cluttered, Wahn,' she said, 'but I didn't have any warning, so there was no time to get things tidied up.'

'Oh, this is just perfect,' replied Wichai, again before Wahn had a chance to open her mouth. 'Thank you so much. It'll only be for two or three nights.' Then turning to Wahn, he added, 'You can put your bags over in that corner.'

Wichai's aunt smiled to herself. 'Make yourselves at home, my dears,' she said. 'Think of it as your own home. I'm going downstairs now.'

As soon as she had disappeared, Wichai went over to where Wahn was standing, with a sad expression on her face. He took her by the arm and led her over to the bed where they sat down. 'You're still frightened of my aunt, aren't you? I've told you, she may look a real old battleaxe, but she's got a heart of gold,' he said, trying to comfort her. 'Just look. Even though she grumbled about it being a bit cramped in here, she's still tried to find us a room apart from the others.'

Afraid that Wichai would think she did not like his aunt, Wahn forced a smile and tried to look cheerful. She looked all round the room, as well as at the bed on which she sat chatting with Wichai. This room was much smaller than the room in the hotel. Apart from the bed, there was a dressing-table, a wardrobe, and various odds and ends which had been turned out, leaving rather a mess. It looked as if the room had previously been occupied by several people. A floral-patterned curtain hung in front of the bed from a bronze-coloured railing, partitioning the room down the middle for privacy.

Wahn and Wichai stayed in the room all that day, until evening, when Wichai's aunt sent some food up to them. When they had finished eating, Wichai suggested that they go out for a walk. Before they left, he took off his diamond ring and gave it to Wahn. 'Put this ring on, too,' he told her, 'so that if we meet any of my family or relatives while we're out, they won't be able to say you're a poor girl.'

Wahn did not reply. She just looked at him with gratitude and kept her feelings of admiration to herself. He was more thoughtful and considerate than she had thought. That evening he took her to see a film, or what they called *nang yeepun* back in Thepharat. She was thrilled by the sight of things she had never before encountered—all the extravagance and splendour of Bangkok, the glittering lights, the streets full of people, cars, and trams. Bangkok was so different from Thepharat, where she would just sit at home dreaming as soon as it got dark. If she wasn't busy cutting the areca nuts and laying them out to dry, ready for chewing, then she would be getting the hemp ready for weaving into mats. Everywhere was pitch-dark. Occasionally, there would be a tonsure ceremony or an ordination in the village. In the distance she would hear the overture of the *pinphat* orchestra. Then she would see neighbours making a commotion, urging the children to light torches and follow them in a file along the dike. Wahn's parents never dared let her go because they were afraid something might happen to her. The most enjoyable time for Wahn was during the rice-threshing or at the merit-making ceremonies at the temple. But these were not a patch on Bangkok. Wahn thoroughly enjoyed her night out with Wichai. However, the moment she returned to the house where they were staying, her spirits flagged.

It was really odd. All the girls in the house dressed up beautifully at night-time and not a single one of them went to bed early. When Wahn got back, she could still see several of them sitting together with a number of men in the front room of the house. Wichai led her up the staircase at the back of the house. They tiptoed quietly to the room his aunt had prepared for them. The sound of a girl laughing softly and a man's voice murmuring something carried through from the next room, startling Wahn.

She turned to him. 'Wichai!' she whispered. 'Wichai, did you hear a man's voice?'

'Yes,' Wichai replied abruptly. 'It sounds like my uncle. Come on in.'

Wahn hurried into the room. That night she scarcely slept because she could still hear the sound of voices and footsteps in the adjoining rooms. Sometimes, just as she was dozing off, she would be woken up suddenly. A man's voice again. This time, however, it was not the same voice that Wichai had said was his uncle's. It was a different man, and he was carrying on as if he was drunk or something. Wahn was on the point of waking Wichai up to ask him what was going on, but she was no fool. She tried to control her feelings and banish the thoughts that were beginning to creep into her mind.

The second and third days passed in much the same way. During the daytime, Wichai hardly stayed with Wahn. He returned only in the evening, when he would take her out for a walk until it was late, and then they would go back together to sleep.

Wichai's aunt saw to it that they were well-fed and looked after. In the daytime, when Wahn was feeling lonely, Samorn would ask her to come out of her room for a chat. Samorn was smart. She would only ever let Wahn talk about her home in Thepharat. The moment Wahn tried to ask her about the strange things that happened every evening in this house, Samorn would put her off and change the subject. On occasions, Samorn told Wahn she was lovely and that it did not seem possible that she came from a family of simple farmers. At other times, Samorn would almost forget herself and say, 'You don't look like a fool, but why...?' and then she'd remember, and stop herself, leaving Wahn puzzled, until....

The fourth night Wichai did not come home and take her out as usual. Instead, he got back late. Wahn was shocked because he came in and promptly flopped down beside her. The smell of alcohol filled the room. She was upset that Wichai had got drunk. Not only was this the first breach of her faith in him as a thoroughly decent man, but also, it made her feel more depressed. She was determined that she would have it out with him the next morning. But when the time actually came, Wahn noticed that he looked upset.

'What's the matter, Wichai?' she asked, unable to bear it. 'You look so worried.'

'Nothing's the matter, dear,' he mumbled. 'It's just that something's cropped up that's bothering me a bit.'

'What on earth is it, to make you look so unhappy?' she asked doubtfully. 'Tell me, so I can help you,' she urged him several times.

'This morning, at ten o'clock,' he replied rather reluctantly, 'a friend invited me to be his best man and to help him take the wedding gifts to the bride's home. I was shocked when I suddenly realized that all my clothes were at my parents' home. I've never been to get them. The ones I've got here are all old and I couldn't possibly wear them. I'd feel ashamed. So I'm not going to bother about being best man.'

Wahn felt sorry for him. When Wichai had taken her out, he had even taken off his diamond ring and given it to her to wear and she still had it. Now that he was supposed to be attending a big occasion, was she going to be so indifferent as to allow her husband to feel ashamed in front of his friends?

'Goodness, is that all the problem is?' she laughed. 'We've got plenty of stuff. There's the gold belt, a bracelet, and a necklace.'

'But they're all yours,' Wichai interrupted before Wahn had finished. It looked as if he was trying to force her into denying it.

'What belongs to a wife belongs to her husband, too,' said Wahn. 'If you think in terms of dividing everything up like this, how can you talk about sharing the ups and downs?'

'No, I didn't mean it that way,' Wichai said, hurriedly excusing himself. 'As a man, I'm embarrassed to have to wear my wife's things. It seems funny.'

'Whoever's going to know they're mine? Go on, take them, please.' Wahn undid her gold belt and laid it down with her necklace. She gave him everything she had brought with her, returning also the diamond ring that Wichai had given her. 'Will you be gone long?' she asked, with a sad look on her face. 'I don't like being all alone. I don't know why. I can't explain it.'

'The bride's house is in Muang Pathum. I'll have to stay overnight, but I'll be back tomorrow night. Now don't go worrying about anything. When I get back, I'll try and sort things out with my parents and ask if we can go back and live in their house. They should have calmed down a bit by then,' he said, trying to reassure her as he dressed. Wahn prepared an overnight bag for him and a moment later he was out of the house and gone.

Wahn spent her time sweeping and scrubbing the room where they stayed. Samorn was very helpful in teaching her to speak correctly, in the same way as people in Bangkok. From time to time, she would come into Wahn's room and they would lie there chatting and keeping each other company. Wahn only came out of her room during the daytime. As soon as darkness fell, she bolted her door and remained inside, alone.

The constant sound of strange men's voices made her wonder why men came here at night. During the daytime, there did not seem to be a single one around, apart from the son of Wichai's aunt. Where they all disappeared to, she had not been able to work out, until the night when Wichai had said he would be back. Wahn waited from dusk until nine o'clock, but still there was no sign of him. She felt restless and could not bear to be in the room any longer. Slowly, she opened the door and stepped outside. She could hear Samorn, Urai, and several others laughing noisily downstairs. She tiptoed down the stairs very quietly, thinking she would ask Samorn about Wichai. Perhaps she would be able to tell her why he had not returned yet. The light in the outer room was bright and through the curtain covering the door, she could see the shadows of people wandering back and forth across the room. She was about to step into the room, when a voice suddenly made her stop dead. She stepped back and hid quietly by the side of the wall. It was the deep booming voice of a man.

'I asked Chao Khun to come with me today, but he said he was going to Pahn Fah.'

Then she heard the voice of Wichai's aunt.

'I suppose they've got a nice little something over at Pahn Fah, then, have they?' she asked. 'And he likes it so much he's forgotten all about us here.'

'Errmm...he did say there are some new faces there, Mae Taht,' the man mumbled, almost apologetically.

Oh! So Wichai's aunt's name was Taht, then. She had only just found out. And those new faces that man had mentioned, what could that mean? Wahn was puzzled. Her face suddenly darkened and she almost fainted on the spot when she heard Ba Taht's mocking voice again.

'A few more days and Chao Khun will be back here again,' she said. 'He may not know it yet,' she added, lowering her voice a little, 'but I'm getting someone new. Waeng's just brought her in from up-country. She's quite a stunner, too. I can see by your face that you think if she's from up-country, she'll smell of mud. This kid's a nice-looking one. But we'll have to wait another two or three days until she's settled.'

Wahn had no intention of listening any further to what was said. Ba Taht's words had made her think that she herself must be the new person in the house, whom Wichai, Ba Taht's own nephew, had brought here. Was Wichai in fact 'Waeng'? Why had the owner of the house spoken like that? The more she thought about it, the more frightened she felt.

The fact that Wichai had not returned as he had promised, leaving her all alone, added considerably to her doubts about why he had left her in this dubious place. However, love made her reluctant to conclude that Wichai could do such a thing.

It was best not to stand around there. She hurried back to her room, her feelings in a turmoil. Ba Taht's words were like a tiny light burning ahead, offering only a blurred vision of the difficulty of her situation. She was about to open the door and go in, but then stopped suddenly because she heard another man's voice coming from one of the girls' rooms right opposite. It was funny that there should be a man messing around in a girl's room at this time. Her curiosity aroused, Wahn tiptoed across to the door. It was closed but not bolted. She leaned forward and peered into the room, which was dimly illuminated by a pale blue light.

What a disgusting sight! There was Prasert with a man. It was not a picture of two young lovers, nor was it as if they were husband and wife. Wahn quickly turned away and fled back to her room, trying to force herself not to think about it. But that was impossible. She could not sleep. She had seen with her own eyes what they were doing, heard with her own ears what they were saying. If things turned out as she feared, then there would be nothing but.... She closed her eyes and shuddered in terror.

Seven

ANOTHER day passed and Wichai had still not returned. Poor Wahn could only wait uneasily. When she asked for news from people at the house, nobody could tell her anything that would ease her unhappiness and suffering. Could all this really be happening to her? When she thought about it, she felt utterly desolate. She sat down in her room, her arms clasped around her knees, and wept. Then she heard footsteps approaching. They stopped outside her door and she heard the sound of the door opening and someone entering. Immediately she thought of Wichai and rushed to her feet, but almost in the same instant, her expression of happiness and welcome became one of sadness and disappointment. The person who had entered the room was none other than the owner of the house, the woman with the cunning face.

'Now then, what are you crying there for, Wahn?' she asked. 'Ob said you hadn't eaten any fish or rice. You'll be ill if you don't eat, and that would make things difficult. And not just for you, either. It would make life awkward for me, too.' For all her apparent concern, she could scarcely conceal her own selfishness.

'I can't eat,' Wahn sobbed. 'I'm worried about Wichai. I don't know why he hasn't returned yet.'

Wichai's aunt laughed as if it were funny. 'Why are you worried about him?' she said. 'He doesn't really love you, dear. And another thing I can tell you: he's not coming back again, you know.'

When Wahn heard this with her own ears, she felt numb with shock even though she already had her doubts.

'Is it really true that Wichai isn't going to come back?' she asked once more to make certain.

'Of course it's true,' the woman replied emphatically. 'What good would it do me to lie to you?'

Trembling, Wahn placed her hands against her breast. 'What am I going to do?' she moaned.

'What are you going to do?' Wichai's aunt retorted. 'Have you got any other relatives in Bangkok?' If you have, you could go and stay with them. Actually, I'm not a relative of Waeng, or Wichai, as he is to you, at all. We just happen to know each other. When he came to ask me to let you stay, he paid for your food and rent, so I was prepared to agree. Now that he's run off, I can't really keep you any longer.'

'I haven't got any relatives here at all, Khun Ba. I'm from up-country. I've only just come here for the first time, so how can I know anyone? I haven't got any money or anything. It's all gone, everything.' As Wahn sobbed, Samorn, who was secretly listening in the next room, also began to cry in pity and sympathy, because she, too, had been through the same thing.

'Well, if you've nowhere to go, you can stay with me. You must understand, Wahn, that I'm not a wealthy person. If you really want to live here, you'll have to help earn your keep.' The last sentence she said with emphasis. 'Of course,' she added, 'if you don't want to stay and you'd rather go somewhere else, that's fine. It's up to you. But don't forget to settle your food and rent first. Think it over carefully.' When she had finished, she left the room, leaving Wahn to grapple with her painful problem.

It was impossible to assess the emotional damage suffered by this young country girl as she was cheated out of all she had, and, what was even worse, brought to this sordid place. When Ba Taht had said 'earn your keep', Wahn had understood pretty well just how you 'earned your keep' there. She was almost beside herself with rage at allowing herself to be tricked into losing her precious virginity, and losing also all her jewellery, each piece of which had only been earned through hard labour. She thought of her parents and brothers.

Were they grief-stricken over her, after the manner in which she had left? Or did they curse her for being a wayward and deceitful daughter? How could she ever go back and face them? If she did go home, she would feel ashamed and people would look down on her and despise her. Her thoughts turned to the man who had betrayed her. How despicable he was, thought Wahn, no longer able to hold back her tears, to deceive an honest girl who loved him so completely.

Samorn quietly came in and sat down beside her. She stroked Wahn's back to comfort her, although her own face was covered with tears. 'That's enough now, Wahn. No more tears.'

This merely made Wahn sob even louder. She pushed Samorn's hand away resentfully. 'I hate everyone who lives here,' she cried angrily. 'I hate everyone who knew all along and yet deceived me.'

Samorn did not take offence and smiled sadly.

'Come on, Wahn, don't be too sad. Crying won't do any good at all. What do you expect me to do? I'm just a nobody, dependent on her, too. Do you think anyone likes seeing someone else going through what you are experiencing now? It would be best to calm down and think things over carefully. Wahn, you're not the only one, you know. I've been through it, too.'

She paused for a moment and noticed that Wahn's sobs had become less frequent. 'It's been even worse for me, Wahn,' she continued. 'Do you think I like living here? Do you think I like being a prostitute? Of course I don't. I'm forced to live this way out of necessity. I've got a husband and a child.'

Slowly, Wahn's curiosity in Samorn's personal affairs was awakened.

'My husband's in prison,' Samorn continued. 'I had no means of earning a living at all. At first, I could earn enough to buy things for him when I visited. But gradually it all ran out, and there wasn't even enough to feed my child. Just think, Wahn, my husband was parted from me, and I had to sell my own child, with his big bright eyes, to get money to buy food for his father. In the end, this is what you have to do. If I didn't, there's no way I could survive and see my husband and child again. Honestly, Wahn, people who don't know despise us. Sometimes they look as if they're disgusted when we walk anywhere near them. You understand, don't you, that we don't like things this way?'

Despite Samorn's tale of hardship, Wahn still did not think that anyone had suffered as much as herself. At least it had provided some temporary relief from her own sorrows. Who was to blame, except herself, for being so foolish? Now that she had lost her reputation, she would have to accept her fate. Sad and embittered, she allowed Ba Taht to push her into the business of 'earning a living'. Many times she tried to put off the evil moment, hoping for some miracle. But for country girls like Wahn, there was no hope and no choice. Eventually, the innocent young girl from up-country changed into what the rest of the world branded a loose woman, a prostitute.

*   *   *

'Wahn' was a rather old-fashioned name. Since she had changed everything else about her life, she decided to take the advice of several people, and change her name as well. So she asked a rather prominent person who frequented Ba Taht's premises and had got to know her well to choose a suitable name for her. It was as if Wahn, the daughter of Ta Kert and Yai Im from Thepharat, had died, and in her place, poor, sweet Reun had been born in the Phraeng Sanphasat area. The long hair, which previously she had tied up on top with a large comb, she now changed to a bobbed style to suit her attractive face and small dark eyebrows which curved over doleful eyes. Instead of a plain *pa nung*, she now wore a close-fitting *pa sin* which showed off her slender figure. She walked, sat, and spoke the way she had seen Bangkok people do. At several other establishments where girls 'earned a living', they could not help looking askance at Ba Taht, who had become proud and haughty now that her premises, which had previously had few customers, had livened up once again.

Reun's new life taught her much. Every night and every day, there were strangers for her to meet, learn from, and gain some deeper understanding. Reun matured quickly and it was probably because of this that from the first moment she met Wit Adinan, she knew that what she felt for him was very different from her attraction to Wichai or 'Waeng'. She could recall clearly the night she first saw him. His was a new face and he was young—about twenty-two or twenty-three. However, what aroused her curiosity was his dignified and manly bearing and his projection of strength and vitality, so utterly different from the puny-looking Khun Wichai. He did not speak loudly and coarsely, nor did he clown about, or get drunk and go wild like other people. He seemed to enjoy just sitting quietly, watching and listening to his friends laughing and joking with the girls. He never became excited beyond the occasional bright smile that would flash briefly in his eyes when he found something amusing. The first time he saw Reun he could not help wondering about her too. When Reun went up to him and asked him if he wanted a soda or orange juice, Wit smiled pleasantly and shook his head.

'What's your name?' he asked. His voice was soft and gentle. All Reun was used to hearing was 'Hey, what's that one's name?' It made her respect him more.

'Reun,' she replied briefly, lowering her head slightly as she spoke.

'Reun,' he repeated softly. He sat thinking for a moment. 'I don't think I've ever seen you before. I suppose you've only just come here?'

'Yes, I've been here just one month.' Wit noticed a sad look come over her face before she replied.

'The month when I didn't come here at all,' Wit said smiling. 'Aren't you feeling very well? You don't look very cheerful.'

She looked up into his kind eyes and then back again at the ground. He was the first man who had taken any personal interest in her. 'It's nothing,' she replied. 'I'm fine.'

'If there's nothing wrong, cheer up and laugh a bit then,' Wit suggested. 'You look as if you're sick of life.'

Reun forced a laugh. From that day, whenever Wit came, he would call Reun over to sit with him. He would tease her and try to cheer her up. There was something about her that was different from the other girls and made him feel protective towards her. The more he listened to Reun talking about her past, the more he felt sorry for her, until finally, his feelings turned into something quite overpowering. Something called love. The number of days Wit spent at Ba Taht's each week increased. He wanted to be near this poor girl so that he could comfort her and give her some hope for life in the future. He loved Reun, loved her so much that he promised he would try to take her away from this place so that they could go and live together as man and wife. She looked upon him as being different from other men. He treated all women with respect, even prostitutes like herself, never looking down on them or regarding them as temporary playthings. He had a strong resolute air about him which was infectious to those near him. The more she respected him, the more her feelings of love towards him increased. He taught her to know the true value of love, even though he himself did not realize how much sacrifice was involved.

After Wit had told her, in all sincerity, that he would take her away to live with him and given her hope that she would one day be his, Reun thought that she ought to keep herself just for him. So she made a special request to Ba Taht that she should not have to go with any other men apart from Wit. This time, unlike in the past, the owner of the establishment raised no objections, because she realized that if she did not agree, Wit might take Reun away, or he might be displeased. It was her job to keep the regular customers satisfied. The ones who gave her a lot of money were the best. Wit only had to come once for her to have enough money to bet on the horses and play cards for several days. Another thing was that she wondered how long it would last. Khun Wit was the son of a wealthy *phaya*. Whatever could he see in Reun? Before very long, he would tire of her and then he would just start looking around for someone else.

Reun, however, did not dare raise her hopes too high that Wit would be able to take her away. He was still at an age when men easily got carried away, when it was difficult to know for sure whether they were really in love or not. Besides, Wit was not just any old penniless fellow. He was from a highly respectable family and he had a growing reputation in society circles. There were likely to be plenty of girls of similar status for him to choose from. How could he be satisfied with her, a worthless prostitute? All she had to offer was a loving and faithful heart, something which was not easy to see, or to show. So Reun could only dream of the day when he would take her away to live in a nice little house. It was something she had wished for, for a long time. She dreamed of being happy and contented, just like any other ordinary wife, and no longer having to force herself to do something as repellent as what she was now doing. Wit had made her aspire to a decent life and provided her with the incentive to get away from all this. He had made her feel that she was gradually becoming a human being again, who could feel joy and happiness when she saw him. But even these feelings were offset by her desire that the future of the man she loved should be bright and successful, and that he should not lose people's respect and become despised because he had come to live with her and quite openly made her his wife. After all, what was she? Just a prostitute.

The word 'prostitute' made Reun sigh heavily as she lay there in silence, her eyes closed and emotionally exhausted. 'Prostitute', 'whore'. The mocking, jeering words echoed in her ears. The happiness that was almost within reach brought with it great torment.

———————— *Eight* ————————

'HARDSHIP,' an observer of human nature once remarked, 'makes men fight harder and awakens ambition in them. It develops their minds and makes them progress in order to escape from that hardship. If there were no hardship at all, what reason would men have for seeking progress?'

Very few people can sit back and put up with hardship. Most will do their utmost to avoid anything unwelcome. On the other hand, happiness breeds laziness and apathy towards work, and makes people bored at the thought of getting on in life. It is as if life and the human course are like a well which has a constant supply of water flowing in and out. The water in the well is the water you can use. If there is water only flowing in, or only flowing out, or if there is water neither flowing in nor flowing out, it would not be called a well.

No one would deny that 'the demise of one thing creates prosperity for another'. But if there are constant demises with no occasion for prosperity, that exceeds the bounds of nature. So it was with Reun's life. While she was wrapped up in dreams of happiness in the near future, some unusual symptoms began to occur, without her realizing it.

One day, Samorn, who had just returned from picking up a dress she had had made, thought she would go and change in the room she shared with Reun. At once she saw Reun sitting there looking pale, with her hand pressed against her chest and a small spittoon in front of her.

'What's the matter, Reun? Have you been sick again?' Samorn asked, putting down the packets she had bought, and hurrying over to rub Reun on her back and neck.

'Yes,' Reun replied with difficulty, before bending over and vomitting again. 'Can you get the *ya hom* in the dressing-table drawer and dissolve it in some water for me, please?'

Samorn quickly rose to do as Reun asked. She rummaged through the dressing-table drawer. 'I can't find it. Oh ... here it is. It was hidden away, right at the bottom of the drawer.' She held the packet of medicine in one hand and wandered around, looking for a glass of water to dissolve it in. 'There's no hot water. I'll have to get some from the kitchen.'

'There's no need for hot water,' said Reun, her hand still pressed tightly against her chest to steady her stomach. 'The cold water in that jug will do. Use that.'

'If you take cold water, it'll just come straight out,' warned Samorn. She leaned out of the window immediately above the kitchen. 'Ob, Ob! Can I have some hot water please? Quickly!'

A voice from the kitchen answered and a few moments later, Samorn got the hot water for the *ya hom*. 'So why are you being sick so often?' she grumbled, dipping a finger into the water to stir it. 'It's once already this morning, isn't it? There ... drink this up,' she added, handing Reun the cup of medicine.

Reun took the cup and swallowed the contents. 'Ah ... that feels better. I felt all funny inside before. I don't know whether I've got a stomach upset or what,' Reun remarked. She took another sip and then lay down in the middle of the spotlessly clean room, resting her head on her right arm. She stared over at Samorn who was hiding herself over in the corner while she took off her blouse and hung it up by the window to dry and then changed out of the brand new *pa sin* she was wearing.

'What did you eat that could have given you a stomach upset? Last night Khun Udom bought up the whole of the noodle vendor's wares and treated everyone. When I called you, you didn't come down. So what did you eat, then, yesterday evening?' Samorn asked crossly, as if she were interrogating a little child.

With her free hand, Reun pulled the spittoon nearer. She nodded and spat out the saliva in her mouth before answering. 'After supper I didn't take anything at all, except a drink of water. I wanted to have noodles last night, as well, but I hate that dirty old drunkard who was with Khun Udom. He talks too much and he can't keep his hands to himself. He was pulling at my hair and pretending he was going to swipe me. He's got no manners, that man.'

Samorn laughed with delight. 'Oh, you mean that old man who's Khun Udom's friend. You haven't seen him when he's sober. He's just like a plank of wood then. He doesn't say a thing. Just sits there blinking.' Having buckled her belt, but still without a blouse on, Samorn went over to where the paper bags and packages she had bought were lying. 'I wasn't going to buy anything today,' she complained as she undid one package. 'Then I popped out for a few moments and now it's all gone. Not a single satang left. And just to make things worse, I get home and find I've got nothing to show for it.' She took some toothpaste, soap, and a toothbrush out

of the bag and put them down on the floor. Then she handed
Reun a paper bag. 'Here you are,' she said. 'I bought some
fruit for you. Are you feeling any better now? If so, try some.'

Reun took the bag and smiled warmly. 'Well, this bag is
something to show for it,' she said. 'By going to the trouble
of buying this for me, you'll have gained a lot of merit,
'Morn.'

'What do you mean, "merit"?' Samorn reproved her. 'I
think of you as my younger sister. I used to have a younger
sister, you know. She is about the same age as you. She's happily settled down now with a husband and kids. She's lovely,
too. That's why when I first saw you, I couldn't help feeling
for you as if you were my own sister.'

Reun smiled again in gratitude. Slowly, she propped herself up and looked inside the bag. What she saw caused her
eyes to open wide in delight. 'Goodness, it's pomelo! Oh,
'Morn, how can I thank you? I could just do with something
a bit sharpish.' She sniffed as she took out a section of the
fruit. She peeled away the white fibre round the outside,
broke off a small piece of the clear segment, and began to
chew it with relish.

Samorn laughed, pleased to see that her efforts were
appreciated. Then, suddenly, she stopped laughing and stared
at Reun sitting there, happily eating the fruit.

'Reun! Stand up a minute,' she ordered, at the same time
getting up herself.

'Here I am, quite happy, and all of a sudden you start asking
me to stand up. OK then.' Still holding a piece of pomelo
and with no idea why Samorn wanted her to stand, Reun
did as she was told.

Samorn's gaze rested on certain parts of the anatomy of
the girl standing before her. Then it shifted and came to rest
suspiciously on Reun's face. A moment later, she bent forward and whispered two or three questions in Reun's ear.

Reun responded with a look of shock and nodded her head.

'Yes. Why do you ask, 'Morn?'

When Samorn heard this quite clearly, she stood there, stunned. The expression in her eyes as she looked at the other girl's face was a mixture of excitement and shock, of pity and doubt. Samorn leaned forward and whispered to her again. This time it was not to ask Reun, but to tell her something.

Reun stopped abruptly. She took a step backwards and put her hands over her stomach, a deep emotion stirring within her. 'Are you sure?' she cried, wanting to be quite certain. She lowered her pale face and looked down at where her hands were resting.

'It must be, Reun, like I said. Being sick, wanting to eat sharp-tasting things, and now ...,' Samorn added emphatically, 'two months. I have been through it, too, you know.'

'Are you sure, 'Morn?' Reun asked once more, as if she did not really know what to say. At that moment, she presented a pitiful sight. She was happy, but fearful and worried at the same time.

'Goodness me,' said Samorn shaking her head. 'I've had a kid before. Believe me.'

Reun felt completely drained when she heard this confirmation. She sank down to the ground and sat there with her head bowed. Her thoughts focused for the first time on her unborn child.

Samorn sat down. 'It's Khun Wit's, isn't it?' she said, unable to refrain from asking.

Reun was shocked by the bluntness of the question. The blood rushed to her cheeks as she nodded in response. But they soon paled again when she heard what Samorn had to say.

'You must hurry up and do something about it, Reun. You can't let it go on like this.'

'What do you mean, "do something about it"?'

'Take medicine so that ...,' Samorn did not finish because Reun had raised her hand to stop her.

'No! I just couldn't do that, 'Morn. I couldn't. I couldn't do it.' She covered her face with her hands in horror.

'So what are you going to do then?' Samorn sounded cross. 'Are you going to let it be born? Perhaps you're forgetting what kind of women we are. Who on earth is going to believe that the child is this person's or that person's? Even Khun Wit. Don't go putting too much faith in him. What will you do if he doesn't accept that he's the father? After all, you're just a prostitute.'

Reun was demoralized. There was nothing she could say. Her maternal instinct had made her happy and excited at the news of what had happened, or what was actually happening to her own blood. But then, what her friend, who had already been a mother, had said made her feel uncertain and caused her to think.

When Reun made no reply, Samorn continued with her warning. 'That's not all, either. All the time we stay here, on these premises, we can't have a baby. It would interfere with work and Ba Taht would cause more trouble. There's no way she would let us stay without getting something out of it, that's for sure. We'll have to leave here if we really want to have a child. Where would you go, Reun? Do you know anyone? You haven't got any relatives. The most important thing is the child would be labelled 'fatherless'.

'It'd be a terrible sin, 'Morn,' moaned Reun. 'I daren't.'

'What do you mean, "a sin"?' demanded Samorn. 'Allowing it to be born when you can't look after it, letting it live in poverty, and then, on top of that, letting people curse it as a bastard—that's what I'd really call a sin. I mean it, now, Reun, are you going to tell the father? Are you going to tell Khun Wit? Come on! Believe me. He's the son of a *phaya*. They're part of the nobility. He's never going to accept that you're the mother of his child. We're prostitutes, remember, Reun. We have to know our place.'

*   *   *

'Prostitute'. The word was razor-sharp, slicing deeply into the heart of Reun, who was now to become a mother. She felt depressed and hurt. Samorn's words set her thinking. All day and all night, with every single breath, she pondered. She waited eagerly for the day when Wit would come. She dared not go round to the front of the house, because in the house just opposite, there was a cute little child whom she had often kept an eye on. Every time she saw the child, Reun felt that she would have liked one of her own. And now, her heart cried out even more for a child of her own, a child she would have with the man she loved and worshipped so much. It would not matter in the least whether it was a boy or a girl; all she wished was that it should be of his blood. It would be a lovely-looking thing with a beautiful face, just like its father, bulging with pale, chubby cheeks. She would love and cherish it and care for it until it was grown up. Even if it wasn't completely like its father, it would at least have some of his ways. Wit's dignified bearing, the firm, resolute note in his voice—these were the things she wanted in her child, this child. Since she wanted all these things so much, could she really just rush off and, utterly cold-heartedly, do something to prevent it being born?

When she was alone, Reun would often murmur to her child as if it were already a human being. 'Darling, I can't do it. No matter how much I love your father, I love you even more. I want you to be my friend in times of trouble.' Sometimes she would break down sobbing when she remembered Samorn's warning that she should never forget that she was a mere prostitute, and not a nice, ordinary girl, pure and untainted enough to be the mother of the aristocratic Wit's child. Even if nobody else would believe that the child was Wit's, she herself was certain that he was the father. What depressed her was that her firm conviction was not shared by any of the others.

She thought about what Wit had said, and his solemn promise to take her away from here to go and live together as man and wife. Her spirits began to revive a little. Perhaps he would believe her, as he had said he loved her. Perhaps he would believe that the child was his own flesh and blood. Wit would be excited and delighted when she whispered the news in his ear. He would be just like other men, who once they have a wife they love, would want to have a child. But then maybe Wit would not believe that she was bearing his child. He would be suspicious. She was a prostitute. A plaything for any passing man. How could she be certain it was his? That is what he would probably think. But surely the fact that she had not been with any other customers for almost three months was a clear enough guarantee by any standards. Reun kept turning things over and over in her mind while waiting for Wit to come and see her again.

But on the night that Wit finally showed up, he looked unusually gloomy. He arrived looking rather distant, like someone with no feelings. When he was close to Reun, he sighed deeply as if he was depressed. This made Reun forget her own problem completely. She moved nearer to him. 'Aren't you well today?' she asked quietly. 'I heard you sighing several times.'

Wit turned away. 'I feel a little unwell,' he lied. 'I think I've got a headache.'

'When you realized you weren't very well, you should have stayed at home and rested. You shouldn't have come. I mean it. I'm not trying to be sarcastic or funny about it. I'm not so awful as to want to see you going backwards and forwards in the rain until you catch a cold. This is the rainy season and lots of people are going down with colds.'

Unable to hold himself back, Wit turned round and gently raising Reun's chin, he gazed down into her deep black eyes. There was a sense of yearning in his words. 'If it had been any other day, maybe I wouldn't have come. But today ...,' he was silent for a moment. 'If I hadn't,' he continued quickly, to cover his trembling voice, 'I just couldn't have stood it.'

Reun laughed brightly, not noticing the state that Wit was in. 'Oh, it's as bad as all that, then, is it? You just wait for me for a minute and I'll go and get some medicine.'

'No, don't, Reun,' he said, raising his hand in protest. 'I don't need any medicine. It'll go by itself.'

Reun, however, was not listening. She smiled as she opened the door. 'It's better to take something,' she insisted. 'I'd feel dreadful if I knew that you were really ill afterwards because I hadn't taken any interest, or hadn't been careful enough.'

Reun returned with a white tablet and a glass of water. When she had prepared it for him, she tried to act cheerfully. She did her best to lift his spirits, even to the extent of forgetting everything she had prepared to say to him. As for Wit, he himself was trying his utmost to be cheerful like Reun, although underneath, his heart ached with sorrow and yearning. It was agony to see her face lying there close beside him, so soft and gentle. As she lay there asleep, he looked closely at her face, at her mouth, her eyebrows, and her chin. He leaned forward and gently and tenderly brushed his lips against her forehead. 'Reun ... oh, Reun. If only you weren't a prostitute,' Wit thought sadly to himself. 'If only. ...'

The next morning, Reun woke before daybreak and urged him to leave, as she had previously. Wit was even more reluctant than usual. More so, in fact, than she had ever seen before. He put on his coat and followed her downstairs. They stood there, leaning against the door, hidden in the dark shadows. Wit appeared to have suddenly remembered something. He put his hand in his pocket and took out a paper packet. He unwrapped the paper and held up the contents for her to see. It was not very dark there and she could see that it was a small gold necklace with an attractive gold locket in the shape of a heart.

'I've got something for you, Reun. Dear me, I very nearly forgot.'

Instead of saying anything, Reun bowed her head against his chest. Gently, he pushed her away a little and then placed the necklace around her neck.

'I'll keep it and look at it when I think of you,' said Reun.

When Wit heard this, his feelings almost got the better of him. He pursed his lips and squeezed the girl's slender hand tightly, holding on to it for some time. Then he gave another sigh and with considerable effort, turned round and walked quickly away.

Wit's unusual haste and abruptness startled Reun. She rushed out after him, and without realizing what she was doing called after him, 'Khun Wit! Khun Wit!'

Silence. There was no response. A flash of lightning momentarily illuminated the dim shadow which had almost reached the end of the lane. The rain, which had been threatening since the previous night, began to drizzle down. It beat against the corrugated iron roof, evoking a feeling of coldness and emptiness. She remained there in a daze for a moment and then turned wearily back into the house, oblivious to the rain which was beginning to fall more heavily. She clutched the locket tightly.

Samorn, who had shown such concern for Reun, emerged from the darkness on the veranda. 'Reun, have you told Khun Wit yet?' she whispered softly.

Reun merely shook her head in response. The hand with which she had been holding on to the bannister suddenly fell away, as if exhausted. But her right hand still clung tightly to something like the heart of the man who had gone. It clung tightly and would not let go.

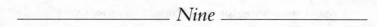

Nine

OUT there on the veranda was not really the best place to talk. She was afraid that other people would find out about what was best kept quiet for the moment, even if it could not be covered up for ever. It was with some difficulty that Samorn tried to keep her curiosity in check as she followed Reun into the bedroom. The door had scarcely closed before she rushed up to her and whispered, 'Why ever didn't you tell him, then, Reun?'

'Khun Wit wasn't very well. He had a headache and he was tired when he first came, so I didn't really like to.' Reun went over to the bed and hung up the front part of the mosquito net by the two brass hooks on either side. She gazed at the pillow where Wit had rested his head. It was still flat where his head had lain. With Samorn still there, she did not dare to bend down and breathe in the lingering scent of his hair and his face, as she had before. So she just sat down on the bed, her legs hanging over the side, and pressed the pillow close to her breast.

'If you didn't like to tell him then, when are you going to?' Samorn demanded. She understood Reun's predicament and felt sorry for her, but she was not one to mince her words.

'Oh, any time I like,' said Reun pretending to laugh as if she was unconcerned. 'You're getting all worked up, 'Morn.'

Samorn walked up and stood directly in front of her. 'Don't go trying to laugh it off in front of me. I know you, only too well. Just you watch out. If you keep on putting it off, you'll end up in trouble one of these days. You won't want to tell him, first for this reason and then for that.'

'What was I supposed to do, then? He came to see me when he wasn't well. He needed a rest and cheering up. It's my job to please him and make him as happy as I can. Next time he comes, I'll tell him. When he's feeling better and his fever has gone. He'll come again in a few days.' Reun tried to rationalize her feelings, but her words were more for her own comfort. This time, when Wit was leaving, his manner had been very different from other occasions. There was a strange empty feeling in her heart. As well as the chain and heart-shaped locket, he had also given her some money before they went to bed. Reun had put it away under her pillow. It had been more than usual, and it made her wonder. Each time, she had got 5 or 6 baht for herself. But this time, the amount had increased to 30 baht. When she had asked Wit about it, he had mumbled that he had got it for some extra work and that it was for her. After that, she had thought no more about it. It was only when he had come to leave, when his manner had seemed rather strange, that she had thought about it again.

She regretted missing the opportunity, the moment she had been waiting for, to tell him what had happened. She wanted to hear what he really felt about it. Would he be excited and delighted that he was going to have a child with the girl he had said he loved and cared about? Or would he be filled with loathing and hatred, and claim that this child was not really his? Reun wanted to hear the answer from Wit's own mouth. But in the end, she had kept on putting off telling him.

What happened after that day did nothing to improve Reun's state of mind. It was just a matter of waiting and waiting. One, two, three days passed. Then seven and eight, and still there was no sign of Wit. Doubt began to grow in Reun's mind. Perhaps Wit had changed his mind. Perhaps he despised her. She tried to think of his good qualities. She thought of the tenderness and sincerity with which he had spoken. Nothing anyone could say would make her think that he despised her. Perhaps he had not been for several days because he was busy looking for a job that would give them a start, so that he could then take her away to live happily together as man and wife. Then her sadness and feeling of helplessness would ease a little, and her mood gradually brighten. In the course of a day, however, it would fluctuate. Her mind would not stay calm for long; the more she thought of the possible seriousness of her difficulties, the more restless she became. She sought feminine refuge in tears. She shut herself up in her room and would not come out to chat with the others, except at mealtimes, when she could eat only a little. She was afraid, moreover, that the others would notice her condition, which she was still keeping a secret. Only Samorn knew the truth, and she had not told anyone.

The agony she was going through over Wit, at least, Reun could stand, no matter how terrible it was. If he really did not intend to take her away with him as he had promised and had decided to run off instead, she could cope with it, when she thought how much she loved him, really loved him from her heart. As a mere prostitute, she loved him in a way that demanded nothing in return. He had been kind enough to take pity on her and to comfort her and raise her spirits. That was more than enough. He had not tricked her out of any money, or deceived her in any way when he left, unlike some of the heartless scoundrels she had met. That day, he had even left with great reluctance, leaving her something as a keepsake and even giving her money to use in times of hardship. She would never find anyone as wonderful as him.

Nevertheless, there were many other things which caused Reun constant pain and anxiety. Her fits of dizziness and vomiting became more frequent so that other people could hardly fail to notice. Furthermore, Ba Taht was always trying to push Reun into entertaining customers as she had before. For the first few days when Wit did not come, Ba Taht had been reluctant to bother Reun, because if Reun was unhappy, she might run away. She would not have had to go far either. If she were to go to a house of a similar nature nearby, it would make things difficult for Ba Taht and considerably affect her income. So Ba Taht tried to keep all of her girls happy. But when Reun would not budge and Wit had stopped coming altogether, she began to nag and threaten her with words that Reun had no wish to hear. If she refused point-blank to go downstairs, she feared that Ba Taht might resort to violence to make her. Who could she turn to, or depend on?

All Reun could do was to keep on waiting, day after day, for Wit to return. But she began slowly to give up hope, because it was coming up to a month since Wit had last been to Ba Taht's house. Some evenings, as she sat chatting alone with Samorn, they would hear a loud knocking at the gate. One such evening Samorn got up and poked her head out of the window. 'Reun! It looks as if it's Wit,' she said happily, but only half certain, as she turned back inside.

Reun's heart missed a beat. The sad expression on her face disappeared, and she immediately brightened. She was laughing and crying at the same time. She rushed over and squeezed up by the window. 'Where? Let me have a look. What's he wearing?'

'I still can't see properly, and Toi's opening the gate slowly, too.' Samorn was just as excited. Her own feelings were affected by what had happened to Reun, as if they were sisters. 'There you are! Oh! It's not Wit, after all. Goodness, he's exactly the same height.'

The blood drained from Reun's face. She leaned against the window sill for support. It was at this time of night that he used to come and see her and be near her and tease her. Where did he go to enjoy himself now? With respectable girls, no doubt. Beautiful, innocent ones, much better than herself. It was only right that he should have that kind of girl for his wife. That way his life would be successful and not in the sorrowful mess it would be if he took a prostitute like herself as his wife. The children born to that girl would receive love and affection as full members of the Adinan family, unlike the tiny baby that she was now going to give birth to. Her baby would come into the world with the heart-searing label 'bastard' or 'son of a whore' attached to it. Tears streamed down her face. She could no longer contain her emotions.

Looking back over her life, Reun felt bitter that all the men she had met had been heartless and unreliable. Clenching her teeth, she tore the necklace she had cherished from her neck and hurled it across the room. There was a loud clatter as the heart-shaped locket and small gold necklace struck the floorboards. Suddenly, it was if she could hear Wit whispering to her softly, as if his lips were pressed close to her ear as he whispered, 'Reun!' Immediately she regretted what she had done. She rushed over to where it lay and carefully picked it up. She gazed down at it as it lay in the palm of her hand, her tears falling on the tiny heart shape. Sobbing silently, she buried her face in her hands.

Samorn watched in astonishment from a distance. This pitiful sight brought back memories of her own past. She had been grief-stricken to the point of suicide that day when the court had imprisoned her husband. The image of that first day they parted, of a man clutching the bars of his cell as he bade farewell to his little child, and then giving Samorn her own freedom, stuck vividly in her mind. Now he lay suffering in a place where there was scarcely day and night, like a caged bird, separated from its mate and young. Even a bird can still cry out in its own way, unlike people who have to keep their sorrows and sufferings to themselves. She thought of him as she gazed at the pitiful sight before her. She sank down to the floor and buried her head against her knees.

That was just one evening. Another evening, Reun was sitting alone in her room, mending some clothes to pass the time. Ba Taht sent Tawin up to bring her downstairs, because there was a new customer, and she wanted Reun to help entertain him. Reun sent Tawin back down to say that she was not very well and that she felt dizzy and had been sick. Ba Taht did actually believe that Reun was unwell, because she had heard Reun vomiting on several occasions in the last two or three days. But she still sent Tawin back up again to ask Reun to come down, even if it was just for a short while. Still Reun refused. Finally, Ba Taht herself went up.

'Go down and look after him for a while, Reun. I've been using up all my energy boasting to him about how beautiful you are, and how nice you are. He's never been to our place before. Go and be nice to him for a bit. If you don't feel up to it today, another day will do. I shan't mind. He's well off, you know. Now, off you go, now, go on. Go and powder your face and do your hair a bit and make yourself look nice. Don't go down looking a mess, because he won't like it and after that he won't come back. He'll be off somewhere else and we'll lose face and that won't do any of us any good.' With a mixture of flattery and encouragement, she tried to cajole Reun into going downstairs to entertain the customer. But Reun still showed signs of reluctance and begged to be excused.

'Now then, dear,' said Ba Taht, who knew what Reun was up to. 'You've been hurt, but you haven't learnt. First, there was Waeng and now it's Khun Wit.' Reun's heart missed a beat when she heard Ba Taht mention his name. 'Well, Khun Wit isn't a bad fellow, like Waeng, but he's from the upper class, with bags of money. What could he possibly see in a working girl? There are plenty of rich girls as it is. He just comes here for a bit of fun and then goes away and forgets about it. He doesn't think about it or dream about it again. And there you are, falling in love with him and saving yourself for him, and all for what? When you do this kind of work, how can you expect to go filling your head with thoughts of love? Forget about it, I tell you. There's no such thing as love for the likes of us. Money, that's all there is. Just money. Remember that, my dear.' As she spoke, she stressed the word, 'money'. 'You can believe me, too. I've let you have it your way lots of times. Now you must help me a bit. So let's see you powdering your face quickly, now, and then you can follow me down. He's waiting below for you.'

Needless to say, Ba Taht's words pierced right through poor Reun. Weakly, she forced herself to her feet and went over to the dressing-table. Instead of powdering her face, she just stood there for a moment before going downstairs, gazing at the thin figure in the mirror. She walked slowly, as if in a trance, paying no attention to the noisy laughter and joking of men and women that was coming from the lounge. She pushed aside the curtain and stepped inside. She stood there in silence and looked over at Ba Taht as if to ask who it was she was supposed to entertain.

As soon as Reun stepped into the room, the laughter suddenly subsided, leaving only the sound of a deep sigh. She was no longer the pale, sad, almost lifeless puppet. Ba Taht signalled with her lips that it was the man sitting on the next chair that she wanted Reun to entertain and the man immediately rose to greet her.

Reun turned her eyes away slowly. Then, slowly, she brought them to rest on the face of the man whom Ba Taht had said, over and again, was wealthy and probably titled. His face was fleshy and his jaws set wide apart. His eyes suggested that he was a man of intelligence, but that he was also cruel and ruthless. He had a strong, muscular physique and his skin was coarse. He laughed loudly, a deep throaty laugh, and approached her in a horrible and frightening manner, like some really repulsive wild beast. As he drew close, he grabbed her by the wrist and held her tightly. She screamed, as if someone had thrown a worm at her. She struggled and then fled through the curtain, slamming the door behind her with a bang and bolting it, as if he was going to pounce on her and grab her. She stood there behind the door, her heart pounding as she gasped for breath. A moment later came the sound of a man's voice, growling deeply, like a fierce beast.

'What's up, then, Miss Beautiful? A bit beneath you, or something, am I? If you don't want to, no one's going to force you. But go slamming the door in my face, and just see what you've got coming to you.'

There was a commotion and what sounded like a table or chair being kicked, followed by the owner's protests and the shouts of the man's companions. 'Please, sir, for my sake, please feel sorry for the girl and have pity on her,' Ba Taht apologized in a trembling voice. 'The kid's nerves aren't so good. She's been a bit round the bend for some time.'

'So why the hell did you make out she was so special?' the man shouted. 'And that she was such a beauty? Huh! The arrogant bitch. What's up with her then? What's the matter with the damn whore?'

'All right, all right. I'll sort things out,' Ba Taht said in a conciliatory tone.

Reun was desperately hurt by the brutish man's words. It was as if they had burned right through her and roasted her heart. 'Damn whore' was what he had called her. She staggered up the stairs and bumped into Samorn, who had been startled by all the noise and was running downstairs to see what was going on. When she saw that it was Reun coming up, her face covered with tears, she realized that Reun must have been the cause of it.

'What's happened now, then? I told you to just keep calm and not go doing anything silly. All the time we stay here, we're in their power. Come on up, now,' she said, half-dragging and half-lifting her into the room. 'Walk properly, or you'll be fainting again in a minute.'

When she had recovered a little, Reun wiped her eyes. 'She wanted me to go with some awful-looking man I've never set eyes on before,' she said, still in a state of some agitation. 'He's been living out in the wilds so long the soles of his feet are like oyster shells. I've never seen anyone like that before. I was absolutely terrified.'

'Now just wait and see,' Samorn warned. 'In a minute that old battleaxe will be here kicking up a rumpus. It really gets you down. Just one thing after another.'

'I tell you, 'Morn, I could kill myself,' Reun sobbed. 'Life's too painful. There's too much hurt. It just goes on and on. I have none of the happiness other people have.'

'Don't think of it that way,' Samorn ordered her. 'Have some pity for the child inside you. Now you've decided you're going to have it, give it the chance to be born.'

Reun moaned softly when she heard Samorn mention her child. Her precious child. The only thing that still made her wretched life worth living. A mother hen looks after her chicks from the time when they are still eggs, protecting them fiercely from anyone who approaches too near. Reun, too, had just the same protective feelings towards the lump of flesh and blood in her body.

Ten

THERE was no doubt, that once the customers had all gone, Ba Taht would indeed 'sort things out' with Reun, as she had promised. On the surface, she seemed cheerful and was making people feel at home. Underneath, however, she was seething with rage. She could scarcely wait for the customers to leave. This bunch of customers, however, did not stay very long, since they were feeling rather annoyed. The man who had caused the incident just sat there looking sullen throughout. As he left, he shouted abusively, 'I shan't be setting foot in this damn hole again,' which infuriated the owner of the premises even more.

Ba Taht had no doubts as to where she would find her temperamental little star, and with great deliberation, she marched up the stairs. Everyone she came across she cursed loudly, irrespective of who it was. Samorn and Reun could hear her quite clearly. It seemed they would not escape her wrath, so Reun pushed Samorn out of the room, not wanting Ba Taht to suspect too much. At least, she still had Samorn to depend on. She sat there, head bowed, awaiting her fate with pounding heart, as if Ba Taht was already in there shouting at her before she had actually appeared.

'I suppose you're hiding yourself away in your room, now, are you, Madam?' Ba Taht opened the door and went in. 'What have you got to say for yourself, then?' she demanded, her voice shaking with fury. 'Are you quite satisfied, now?' Reun remained silent, her head lowered.

'It's all the same, whether I'm strict or whether I go easy on you. Do you want me to really sort you out? You go putting on airs and playing hard to get, and then the more I try to be nice to you, the more arrogant you get. I told you, right from the start, that if you stayed here, you had to help earn your keep. How can you expect to go picking and choosing like that? My godfathers! There you are, waiting for Khun Wit, and you're only going to go with Khun Wit, because you're his favourite.... Huh!' She gave a loud, mocking laugh. 'And has he been to see you, then, eh?'

'Please don't go bringing other people into it,' Reun protested in a trembling voice, no longer able to keep her silence. 'If you want to curse someone, then curse me alone, or beat me, if you want. I won't complain. I admit that I was wrong to behave badly in front of other people.'

On hearing Reun's admission, Ba Taht's fury abated a little, although she was still very annoyed. 'What was so bad about him that you had to go and do that? Wasn't he good-looking enough for you? Or was it that he didn't look like your lover? I told you, I did, before you went down, to be nice to him, and that he's got plenty of money and that later he'd be falling for you. But goodness me, there you go, making such a song and dance about it, as if he were an ogre, or the devil, or something. Haven't you ever seen anyone like that where you come from? Have you only ever come across slim-hipped, slender-waisted fellows like old Waeng and that favourite of yours, Khun ...?' She did not mention Wit's name, but simply stood there, rubbing her hands together and trembling with rage. 'You make me sick, you do.'

'No, I really haven't, Ba,' Reun replied in all honesty, shuddering in disgust at the thought of the man. 'Not anyone that looked like that. Before I knew what was going on, he'd rushed up and grabbed my hand.'

'So what's so special about you, then,' Ba Taht yelled, 'that he should have to come bowing and scraping to you? Just you wait and see. Tomorrow, I'm going to make you start working. I've let you have your own way for a long time and it seems to have gone to your head.'

'Oh, dear,' said Reun. 'I'm really not well, honestly. You can see for yourself. Wait till I'm a little bit better, please.' She pleaded stubbornly in the hope of putting it off, although she had no idea what the future would hold.

'I'm not waiting any longer. I've already waited, lots of times. It's like waiting for the cows to come home. Aren't you even the least bit embarrassed at staying here, eating and sleeping here without giving me a single bit of help as far as earning some money is concerned?'

Before, when Reun had first gone to stay there, she was not familiar with the way things were there. She had allowed herself to be intimidated, slapped, and cursed and she had been forced to do what Ba Taht wanted. But now, the bruising she had taken and the coercion she had been subjected to had toughened her sufficiently to stand up to any new adversity. As a result, her expression changed immediately. She stared at the owner of the house, who was seething with rage, and instead of pleading and begging for sympathy and kindness, she replied in a clear voice. 'You are my elder, yet aren't you even the least bit ashamed? When I'm not sick, I make more money for you than all the others. And it's not just from Khun Wit, either, who gives you plenty of money whenever he comes. There are plenty of others, too, you seem to forget. Now you come pressuring me when I'm not well. Just think about it. Whoever's going to want a sick, pale-looking girl like me? People want to come and relax and enjoy themselves. They want to chat and joke about with fresh-looking girls. If you go driving a sick person down to entertain them, you'll just be damaging your own reputation.'

Ba Taht was silent for a moment, wide-eyed with astonishment. Every single word that had poured forth from Reun's mouth was true and Ba Taht had only just realized it. But she could not allow some young girl to go raising her voice to her for fear of being shamed, so when Reun paused for breath, she interrupted in a loud voice. 'And how many months, is it, my little darling, since you went with someone else?' she demanded sarcastically.

'There's no need to go calling me "little darling". At the moment, you know I haven't been as much use to you as you would have liked. I know perfectly well how many months it is since I last went with someone. I also know how many months the money you get from the people I go with should cover. It's only for just over a month that you haven't been getting very much.' She took some money out from under her pillow and handed Ba Taht 10 baht from the 30 which Wit had given her. 'Maybe this will be enough for little Toi's school fees next term. I heard him asking for it yesterday morning. You're funny, you know, Ba. Your own child, you love and take care of and you find the money for him to study because you want him to be successful in the future. And then you come squeezing the money out of the girls, forcing them to do this shameful job, without a moment's rest. And when anyone gets ill, you won't even believe them. Toi might well be someone high up one day, as you hope, but no one will know as well as I do about his former life, and that he made it on the money which prostitutes like us sweated our guts out for. Prostitutes everyone despises. Yes. Damned prostitutes.'

Yes, indeed. Provoking a quiet person can often lead to trouble and Reun was no exception. Several of the other girls, Samorn included, who were sitting outside listening, felt, for the first time, a sudden wave of anger when they thought of their own plight. It was true. Ba Taht really was exploiting them. Her son she loved. But she forced them to work day and night.

Reun's words prompted Ba Taht to snatch the money and leave the room quickly. Money was all she wanted. She could not care less what people said, but Reun's words had angered her because the other girls were beginning to get a little troublesome. If they did not feel like it, they would start being stubborn and insist that they were unwell, too. And if she said anything, they would simply say, 'Why is it all right for Reun?' and 'It's all right for me, too, then.' Ba Taht felt more and more frustrated. Reun had undermined her absolute authority within the house. She was like a speck of dust in Ba Taht's eye, a painful irritation which could not be dislodged.

Reun was only too well aware that the 10 baht she had given Ba Taht would merely put off the evil moment for a short while. Once the money was all gone, Ba Taht would be back again, pestering and cursing her. While Reun was still trying desperately to think what to do next, Samorn came in looking worried.

'It's no good, Reun,' she said. 'Looks as if Win knows, or something. A moment ago she said, 'What's the matter with Reun? She keeps throwing up and getting a craving for sour things.'

'What did you tell her?' Reun asked with concern.

'I said I didn't know,' replied Samorn. 'Reun, hurry up and get things sorted out.'

'Get what sorted out?' Reun asked, feeling disheartened and near her wits' end. 'Help me think of something.'

'So now you want me to help you, then. I told you to sort things out so that it wouldn't be born, before it became flesh and blood. But you're still hanging about waiting. Now do you see how serious things are?' Samorn demanded, like an adult scolding a child.

'Goodness, 'Morn, you know the way I feel. Have a bit of sympathy for me,' Reun said in a trembling voice.

'It's because I feel sorry for you,' said Samorn, 'that I feel so depressed. I can't eat or sleep, either. What are we going to do?'

Reun's face looked even sadder than before. 'What else can I do, except leave here?'

'And go and live where?' Samorn asked sullenly.

'That's the problem. I don't know anyone. Not a single person. If I did, I could go and stay with them, and maybe work for them,' Reun mumbled.

'What could you do?' There was pity in Samorn's voice. She glanced over at Reun's figure. It made her even more depressed that certain parts of Reun's anatomy might make people suspect or actually realize.

'Ironing, washing, sweeping around the house. I could do all these things and do them well. But I can only cook simple food—the way we used to eat back home,' she replied truth-fully.

Her companion sat frowning thoughfully for a moment as she tried to think of someone she could send Reun off to work for. She remembered someone she used to know who was now married to a high-ranking *khun nang*. Her house was very big and there were lots of people there and plenty of work to do. Perhaps she needed a bit more assistance. Another thing was she did not know anything about Reun's back-ground. It was worth a try. Quickly, she told Reun about it.

That very same day, Samorn managed to get away from the house. She went straight to the home of the girl she used to know, and then returned to Reun with news of her success.

'It's all arranged, Reun. She's short of a laundry maid, so I told her I knew a girl—that's you—who was looking for a job. I hope you won't be angry with me. I told her that your husband was dead and that you didn't know what you were going to live on so that she'd feel sorry for you.'

Reun was delighted to be leaving this house, leaving for a new life. But her face dropped a little at the words, 'your husband is dead'. Then she thought it was better to think of him as dead, rather than to think anything else that might make her feel hurt. She forced a soft laugh. 'Where's her house, then?'

'It's on Sukhothai Road. Ask for Luang Pha-ngaht-cherngyut's house. He's an army officer. Everyone knows him. His wife's name is Bunnag.'

'What time did you tell her I'd go?' Reun asked.

'Tomorrow night, about nine o'clock. She wondered a bit about why you were going to be so late, so I told her you didn't want your mother-in-law to see you. Oh, and I told her how difficult things have been for you so that she'd be nicer to you,' Samorn said with amusement.

'Will you take me there?' Reun asked.

'How can I? If I did, Ba Taht would kill me. But don't worry, Reun. When you get out of here, take a rickshaw and tell the fellow to go to Sukhothai Road by the front of Wachira Hospital.'

'What hospital?'

'Wachira. And then you get off and ask for Luang Pha-ngaht, the army officer. Everyone knows him.'

Reun heaved a great sigh of relief. Tomorrow night she would leave this house and escape from all this sordidness. Then she thought of Samorn and her expression at once became sad. 'I'll really miss you,' she said softly.

'Don't worry. I'll come and see you often,' Samorn said, bringing the conversation to an end.

After that, Reun secretly gathered her things together and put them in a bag, making sure that she had only those things which were really hers. There was still some money left over after paying Ba Taht, and she took this with her. In addition, Samorn had given her the money she herself had been trying to save. Reun was reluctant to accept but Samorn insisted and stuffed it into Reun's bag.

On the evening she was to leave, Reun put on a cheerful face and went down and, unlike previous days, sat around chatting brightly, helping Ba Taht to entertain the customers. Ba Taht herself had been beginning to wonder about Reun's frequent bouts of sickness, and several people had been whispering things in her ear. But now she forgot all that and chatted amiably. Reun would certainly help her bring in a bit of money today.

Customers had been arriving since the early evening. They were nearly all regulars and not exactly quiet, either. One group had brought a gramophone and records along, and the moment they arrived, they sent Toi off to buy some whisky and soda. Then they moved some of the chairs out of the living-room and others over to the side of the wall so that they could practise the new style of dancing, where everyone seemed to be all mixed up together. All the girls, except Reun, were having a good time with the young men. She alone felt nervous. She stole an anxious look at Samorn, but she looked quite pleased, because all this noise provided a much better chance of escape than if all had been quiet. The young man's wrist-watch showed eight o'clock. She had no chance of slipping away yet, because it was many months since she had seen this bunch, and they kept asking her over to chat, so that she scarcely had a free moment. It was funny to think that this was her last time in this house. Who would have known? Reun laughed softly. Then she laughed again, a loud, clear laugh that echoed across the room. Samorn alone knew what that laugh meant. Reun lowered her head quickly and swallowed hard, making a strangely cold, piercing sound.

Ba Taht was busy fixing the *naem* and other snacks which the group of rowdy young men had ordered to eat with their whisky. As Samorn went over to lend a hand, she glanced sideways at Reun to let her know that she should be on her way. Reun was sitting winding up the gramophone. She let go of the handle immediately and asked a young man sitting there with eyes bloodshot from the alcohol to take over, telling him she would be back in a minute. Then she walked past Ba Taht and out of the room. She stopped for a moment and stood looking into Samorn's eyes as if to say goodbye. But when she saw Samorn scowling at her, as if to hurry her up, she quickly went upstairs and grabbed the bag in her room. Just as she was about to leave the room, she stopped suddenly and stood there in silence. She put her bag down and went over to the bed. Then she flung herself down, sobbing with grief.

She lay on the same spot where Wit had lain, whenever he had been to see her. Wit, the man who had taught her the true value of love, the man she loved more than anyone, the man who meant everything to her, had lain next to her on that very spot. His face, his appearance, everything about him was still vivid in her mind. When Wit had stopped coming, she had lain crying on the same pillow where he had lain. Here, in this room with Wit, she had been happy. From now on, she thought, sobbing as she buried her face in the mattress, she would never see it again, never stay here again, and never lie weeping here, as she had done every single day and night.

Anyway, what good did it do, getting so upset? Reluctantly, she rose from the bed and went slowly over to where her bag was. She picked it up, as if all the strength had drained from her, and tiptoed quietly down the stairs and out of the door at the back of the building. She skirted her way round to the front and carefully, so as not to make a noise, she undid the lock. She stepped outside and stood in the darkened road. She looked back once more at the bright lights in the house. She could hear the sound of laughter, of men and women mingling together, the clinking of glasses, and the sound of shoes, dragging across the wooden floorboards in time to the music which issued from the gramophone, as the needle worked its way down to the final groove of the spinning record. She looked up at the window of her room, as if to say goodbye for the last time. Then, lowering her head, she hurried away from Phraeng Sanphasat.

She found a rickshaw parked at the end of the road. The Chinese owner was sitting on the footrest, fanning himself with his hat. Seeing the girl walking towards him, he got up to have a look. Reun stepped straight into the rickshaw and put her bag on the floor. 'Sukhothai Road,' she ordered, 'in front of Wachira Hospital.' The rickshaw took Reun off on a lengthy journey along various streets, turning down one way and then emerging from another. Passers-by stared at the pale-looking girl sitting there, but she was oblivious to everything except the monotonous rhythmical patter of the Chinese man's shoes on the gravel as he pulled the rickshaw along.

Eleven

LUANG Pha-ngaht's house was a large, hip-roofed building on Sukhothai Road surrounded by a tall hedge. At the front of the house was a small lawn on which a badminton court had been marked out, so that his children could bring their friends over to play there in the evenings. Beyond the main building, stretching out in a row as wide as the house, were the kitchen and servants' quarters. These were divided into individual rooms with two people occupying each one. Although the house looked big, when you actually went inside and saw the general state of it, you could not help feeling that it was rather cramped for Luang Pha-ngaht and his wife and their three daughters and two sons. Some of the daughters went out to work and earned a small salary, while the rest were still at the stage of whinging and getting themselves into trouble. In addition, there were Luang Pha-ngaht's mother, who was a crotchety, rather forgetful old lady, her carefree young nephew, and a distant female cousin of Luang Pha-ngaht's wife, all living under the same roof.

As soon as morning came, there would be a terrible commotion and confusion throughout the house, which began with getting the children off to work or school. One person's clothes would be missing, another's books would have gone astray, and they would be fighting and quarrelling until their father, who liked to lie in and go to work late, would suddenly emerge from his mosquito net and call out to their mother. She would then pick up a slender rod and beat the younger children two or three times, whereupon they would see who could cry the loudest. When she heard the children crying, the grandmother would emerge awkwardly from the room where they kept most of their antiques, such as betel bowls, earthen jars, and Lao bowls, and start grumbling about her daughter-in-law only beating the children because she did not want her husband's mother living in the same house. When the nephew returned from his early morning stroll and heard all the fuss, he would go straight over to the gramophone and pick out the loudest record there, so adding further to the din. The neighbours could barely stand it, but there was nothing they could do except put up with it first thing in the morning. Later, things would quieten down, but only until the latter part of the afternoon, when the children invited their friends round. Then there would be shouting and laughter and the sound of racquets striking a shuttlecock until it was dark. At ten o'clock at night, the house was at its quietest.

Reun had settled in as a maid. It was her job to do the washing and ironing and help the cook. She worked with Sa-aht, another young girl, who carried out general duties for everyone, including sweeping and cleaning the house. During the first few days, the disturbance almost drove Reun mad, but as she had nowhere else to go, she had to stick her head down and carry on working, so as to have somewhere to stay. Food was provided, so she did not have to go out and buy it. The laundry kept her busy nearly all day long and she hardly had time to go and help the cook. Her bouts of vomiting had not completely passed and some days she had to rely on her honest face and gentle manner to arouse pity in her employers in order to gain some respite.

Before daybreak, she got up and went to the kitchen to help Mae In to prepare breakfast. She would wipe the plates and bowls and spoons and forks, or else she might slice up the vegetables. When she saw people in the house were awake, she would go up and help with the cleaning, put out the clothes they were going to wear to work or school, and gather up the dirty washing. She washed and ironed every day. There were never less than three garments for each of the male members, and even more for the girls, what with going-out clothes, sports clothes, nightdresses, and other odds and ends. However, they were easy to wash and not very dirty. There were not so many things to wash for the little boys, but their clothes were covered in dirt and sweat and were really hard to clean. For the grandmother, there were the fewest things of all. Just one blouse every two days, except that she had to use lime to scrub the betel juice stains out. For Khun Luang, there was an army uniform, which, she was relieved, was sent out to a Chinese laundryman. Then there were his wife's and younger sister's *pa lai*, which had to be starched and pressed.

*   *   *

Kept busy at the back of the house, Reun scarcely ever went round to the front. Every afternoon, Sa-aht had to rush about buying ice and orange juice and preparing snacks for the regular group of badminton players. Every day they wore themselves out this way until a whole month had passed and Reun was given her salary of 5 baht to add to the money which Wit had given her. One result of so much work was that Reun had no time to sit around thinking about him and feeling sad. All she could think of was work and her own duties. In the evenings, when she had finished work, she fell asleep, exhausted, the moment her head touched the pillow. Such was life as she had already experienced it; there would be still more she would have to go through in the future.

One day Sa-aht caught a cold. She woke with a temperature and was unable to get up and carry out her duties. She just lay there, feverish, in her room. Luang Pha-ngaht's wife ordered Reun to take over all of Sa-aht's duties and to forget about the laundry for a day. So from early morning, Reun carried out her new tasks, running around after the little ones, who were at home because it was Sunday, sweeping the house, and tidying up the bedrooms. In the afternoon, she carried the basket for Grandma when she went shopping for fruit and cakes at Saphan Han and Bangrak. Grandma told her that there would be several newcomers coming to play badminton today, so she would have to prepare the fruit and snacks especially nicely.

'You'd better help me set up the refreshment table on the lawn, Reun. Sa-aht's not very well,' Grandma said, before they reached home.

Reun was quick to obey. She rushed about all the time while the guests were arriving. That day there were several new faces among the young men and women. Reun carried out Sa-aht's duties efficiently. She took the fruit juice out and served all the guests without taking any notice of what they looked like, or whether they were beautiful or not. When she had finished serving the orange juice, she went into the house and emerged with the fruit basket. Before she had reached the lawn, Grandma came up to her, calling out that another guest had just arrived and wanted orange juice. Reun put the fruit basket down, placed the orange juice on a small tray with a glass, and walked over to the lawn. Grandma pointed to the edge at the far end of the lawn, and said, 'Give it to that man over there. The one sitting with his back to us, in grey shorts.'

Reun looked over in the direction that Grandma was indicating and then walked straight towards the man. When she reached him, she leaned forward and gave him the tray with the orange juice. The man was chatting away loudly. His voice sounded familiar. She looked up at him just as he turned round to take the glass of orange juice.

'Khun Udom!' The words slipped out of Reun's mouth before she had even realized it. She recovered herself and bowed her head in silence, her hands shaking violently.

'Reun!' cried Udom simultaneously in surprise. He was a regular at Ba Taht's. He quickly took the glass of orange juice, and then, full of curiosity, asked, 'What are you doing here?'

'I work here,' she replied, and immediately hurried back, leaving Udom staring after her in astonishment, wondering how Reun, a prostitute from Phraeng Sanphasat, could be mingling among those in this household, a household in which there were lots of young girls. When he had asked for Reun, Ba Taht told him that she had run away. So Reun had run away from Ba Taht's and come to work at Luang Pha-ngaht's house. It was certainly strange. Reun thought as much, too. She was worried that if Khun Udom made any mention of it to the owner of the house, then she would be driven out immediately, because she had been a prostitute. Her employer was bound to disapprove. Besides, that was not all, for he might think that she was up to no good in this house. However, the day passed safely, and Udom did not say a word. He just watched her closely all the time as she served the visitors.

Early the next morning, Samorn came to see her. When Reun saw her face, she felt depressed and nervous and frightened. They had scarcely sat down before Samorn whispered, 'You can't stay here, Reun. Last night Khun Udom was telling everyone he'd bumped into you working here. Ba Taht was cursing you and swearing about you.... Why did you let that gossip, Khun Udom, see you?'

'I didn't intend to let him see me. You wouldn't get me showing my face outside with him in a million years. I just happened to be unlucky, yesterday.' And Reun told Samorn how it had happened.

Samorn sighed out of annoyance. 'You'll have to go somewhere else. Don't wait for them to drive you away. This is the last time I'm coming here. I daren't come again. Khun Udom is bound to say something. On top of that, Ba Taht is saying you stole some of her things.'

'Oh my goodness! She's accusing me of stealing her things, 'Morn?' Reun was shocked. 'Good Lord, I never took anything of hers. Not a single thing. I didn't even bring all my own things with me.'

'It's a waste of time talking about it. No one will believe us. You've got to leave today. If you hang about, there'll only be more trouble,' Samorn said quickly, scarcely pausing for breath.

'Where can I go?' Reun asked in bewilderment.

'Look, I said you've got to go, so let's go. Get your things together and go and tell the lady of the house you're leaving now. I've already told her, just a minute ago, that I was taking you to stay somewhere else.' Samorn spoke as if she really was Reun's elder sister and Reun did as she was told. She packed her bag once more and set off again, as fate would have it.

The place Samorn took her to was Ratchadamnoen Nork Road. It was just a small house on its own, painted green. The owner was a young woman of about twenty-seven. Just one look was enough to tell Reun what kind of business she was in. She was pale, like other girls Reun had seen so often, and she dressed differently from ordinary women and had certain mannerisms in common with others of her type. Kesorn operated at the top level. She had her own house and money, which she got from offering her services to wealthy men. It was with this same Kesorn that Samorn had found work for Reun, as a maid, doing all the jobs around the house, except cooking, for which she would receive 5 baht a month.

Kesorn's house was a bit better in that there was not the noise and chaos there had been in Luang Pha–ngaht's house. But Reun had to endure Kesorn's threats and tongue-lashings whenever she did something too slowly, or which displeased her employer. Reun's speed and nimbleness were gradually deserting her and her movements became increasingly slow and ponderous. When she was in the middle of doing one thing, Kesorn would call her to come and do something else, and if she was not quick enough, Kesorn would scold her angrily. There was less work and there were not so many clothes to wash as there had been in the other house. At night, however, there were frequent visitors and she had no time to rest. If some rich man came to take Kesorn out, that was when Reun had some time off.

Reun would spend such times sitting quietly in the dark, gazing absent-mindedly out of the window. It was not the cars and other vehicles running up and down Ratchadamnoen Road, nor the boys and girls who sat chatting or going about their business, that held Reun's gaze at such times; she simply stared aimlessly. Sometimes the row of tamarind trees which stretched out in a long dark line before her reminded her of the *sakae* trees on either side of Khlong Prawet, which stretched out as far as the eye could see, beyond Thepharat District and out to the Bang Pakong River at the Tha Thua

Dam. The only difference was that the tamarind trees on either side of Ratchadamnoen Road were tended by workers who trimmed them so that they were the same size all the way down the long row, while the *sakae* trees that lined the banks of the canal had no one to look after them. Some towered out above the others, their branches stretching out like animals crouching or walking slowly. Occasionally, the dark shadows of densely foliated banyan trees could be glimpsed, spreading their branches down into the canal.

The rainy season had almost passed. It was getting cooler now and there were gentle breezes. She thought of the cool season back home where she was born. In the evenings, by this time, the whole family used to be sitting around the fire, warming the palms and backs of their hands, while her mischievous little brother would poke taros into the fire with a stick. Mother would quietly tell them what she could remember of the Jataka tales she had once heard from the monks at the temple on holy days. Father would squat down on his heels and huddle up under a large blanket. He did not pay the least attention to the story because he would be worrying about Ai Peu-ak and Ee Taen, the buffaloes, who were pacing restlessly in their enclosure next to the house because of the cold. Occasionally, he would look up and crane his neck to see if the fire which he had lit beside their enclosure had gone out. If it had, he would call Reun's elder brother, who would be sitting mending his fishing rods, to go and see to it for him.

With her daughter missing, Mother probably did not tell any stories because there would be no one sitting there, badgering her. Her younger brother probably did not get much fun out of tossing taros or cassava on to the fire, and with no one trying to snatch them away, the sweet-smelling taros would no longer taste so good. Sitting on the jetty, her elder brother would gaze drowsily down the canal, as far as the eye could see, staring at the fish, large and small, snapping at the bait in front of him. There was no point in casting his net or trying to lure them on to his hooks. There was no one to help him paddle the boat now, nor anyone to dry out and salt the catch. Her palm-leaf hat and sickle would be left there untouched, the hat gathering a coating of soot, while the sickle, once so sharp, as it cut through the rice heads during the harvesting season, would now be turning rusty. Mother would have to go to the kitchen herself to get the rice and curry to offer to the monks. Sometimes, when there had been nothing to eat with the rice, Reun used to run off to a neighbour's house and ask for young luffa gourds to make *gaeng liang*; or else she might go and pick young tamarind leaves, to boil with the heads of *pla chorn* fish, and they would grill salted fish until they were yellow all over. Then they used to dish out the bowls of rice and sit round savouring the meal. Now it was probably quiet and empty. They probably sat around inside, brooding in silence. Maybe they were worried about their runaway daughter. Maybe they had cut her off and no longer cared. A tear dropped on to her hand, startling her.

*   *   *

Some days when Reun was working for Kesorn, she would be too slow in her work and would be cursed and shouted at. She felt hurt by this and it made her cry. Back home, even if it was rather rural and unsophisticated compared with the city, no one dared to speak to anyone else in such a hurtful way, but when things had been good, she had not liked it and had gone and brought pain and suffering upon herself. Before she had time to dry her eyes, Kesorn glanced over in her direction, and delivered an ill-tempered rebuke.

'What's all this, then? I only have to open my mouth and you go bursting into tears. Are you really that sensitive? If you're afraid it's beneath you, don't bother to take up the job.'

'No, Ma'am, I've never thought that at all,' Reun sobbed, lowering her head and folding the dozen or so dresses that Kesorn had pulled out and thrown in a pile in front of the wardrobe.

'So what's on your mind, then? It's your fellow, is it? What do you want to go bothering yourself with him for, when he's left you? He's not worth getting upset over. You never want to go falling in love with a man. Just take me. Now there's no way I'm going to love any man. If he's got money, he's more than welcome to take me wherever he wants. Why did you have to go and get yourself a whinging little kid? Once you've got one, you won't be able to find it a father. Just look at you, Reun. If it weren't for 'Morn, I wouldn't be wasting my money employing you. You're a nuisance, wandering around with a belly that size. I feel embarrassed in front of visitors. As for the work you do, it's not worth the money. Just look at this dress here. I told you to get it ready yesterday, but you haven't.'

Kesorn's words were like boiling water being poured over Reun's heart. She gritted her teeth and fought back the tears. She had arranged the clothes in the wardrobe yesterday, but they were untidy again because last night, Kesorn had pulled them all out when she was looking for the one she wanted to wear when she went out. Reun opened her mouth to protest. Then she thought of Samorn having to run around looking for another place. It would be a lot of trouble for Samorn. So she kept quiet and suffered the bitter-sweet flavour of the situation.

Another evening, Kesorn sent Reun to buy food at Ratchawong. When Reun returned, at about nine o'clock, she saw a car parked under the dark shadows of the malabar almond tree in front of the house. There was a light shining in the dining-room. Kesorn must have a visitor, Reun thought as she made a detour round the back way. She went up the steps and into Kesorn's room. Kesorn, who was hurriedly getting dressed, caught sight of Reun in the mirror and called out to her. 'Put them down there, Reun. I'm not going to eat yet. Can you get a drink for the gentleman waiting in the other room?'

Reun quickly set about carrying out her orders. Carefully, she carried a glass of water into the living-room. The man was sitting with his legs crossed and a newspaper held up in front of his face. Hearing footsteps approaching, and thinking it was Kesorn, he lowered his newspaper and smiled. His smile startled her so much that she almost fainted. At first glance, he looked just like Khun Wit, but as the smile faded and gave way to a look of astonishment, Reun pulled herself together. She lowered her eyes and placed the glass of water on the little table in front of him, with a visibly trembling hand.

The man shifted his position. 'What's your name?' he demanded.

'Reun,' she replied in a shaking voice. This was not someone she wanted to meet. Wit had not spoken to her in such a harsh tone the first time he had met her. She could still remember the first time they had met and he had asked her what her name was.

'Why did you look so startled when you saw me?' the man continued abruptly, looking her up and down in a condescending manner. He was better-looking than Kesorn, but he spoke in a throaty, rather emotionless voice. Khun Wit had never stared at her in such a way, Reun thought.

'Because you look like someone that a lowly servant like me once knew,' she replied abruptly and then turned round and left the room, passing Kesorn in the doorway.

Even though the man who had come to take Kesorn out had behaved in a haughty fashion towards her, Reun was still glad to steal a look at him as he got up and walked out, side by side, with Kesorn, to the car. Reun watched him until he disappeared from sight. In some ways he looked so like her Wit. She buried her head in her arms, among the furtive shadows. Where had her darling strayed off to, leaving his wife to endure hardship and heartache as she wandered trance-like from one place to another? Reun laughed through her tears. 'Reun's a prostitute,' she murmured. 'How could she be your wife?'

Twelve

IN the spacious paupers' maternity ward, the patients' beds numbered more than ten. They were arranged in rows and suitably spaced apart, with the head against the wall and sufficient room at the end for the doctors and nurses to make their rounds. The patient in the bed nearest the entrance was a middle-aged woman who looked as if she worked in the fruit orchards. She lay there with her eyes closed, groaning in pain from something internal. She had just had an operation. Next to her was a Cantonese woman, who lay with her eyes wide open, weeping over the child she had just given birth to, but which had since died. She kept moving restlessly, disturbing another woman who was lying quietly, only occasionally opening her eyes, for she was still weak from the loss of blood, having given birth the previous evening. The warm morning sunlight flooded into the building. Bright rays pierced through the glass windows and penetrated as far back as the wall where Reun's bed was, making her pale face and long, curling eyelashes a rather pitiful sight.

At that moment, Reun wanted nothing more than to see the child she had not yet had the chance to set eyes on. She had heard its fierce little cry only once, and then all had been quiet. She tried to contain her frustration for a while by looking round at her fellow patients. As far as she could make out, the beds were nearly all occupied by patients who were in a bad way. The one on her right, however, had almost recovered, and was able to sit up. Chatting to one or two of the other women, Reun learned that the Chinese woman, lying there moaning in a language nobody could understand, had lost her child three days after it was born. Reun could not help wondering about her own child. She wanted to see it, to know whether it was a boy or a girl, to know that it was alive. The continuous moaning and groaning echoing in her ears only made Reun feel worse. Fortunately, just when she could scarcely stand it any longer, the nurse on duty came in carrying the newborn infants, tightly wrapped in white, freshly laundered shawls. All that was visible, as the nurse approached, were the round faces and mass of thick black hair. She looked competent and skilful, carrying two babies at the same time. One, she gave to its mother, further down the room, while the other, she handed to Reun.

'Is it a boy or a girl?' Reun asked in a shaky voice as she held out trembling hands to take the baby.

'It's a girl, my dear,' the nurse replied. 'A horrible, ugly little girl, just like its mother.'* She glanced sympathetically at the mother's face. 'Reun' was a nice name, she thought, as she went off to carry out her other duties, and the mother was still young and beautiful.

With her little baby in her arms, Reun was so overjoyed that tears streamed down her cheeks. She was no longer concerned for the Chinese woman, who had stopped her loud wailing and now looked on dazed at the sight of mother and child. Then she turned away and began to cry again, thinking

---

*Traditionally, adults make such disparaging remarks to discourage evil spirits from laying claim to a newborn child.

of the child she no longer had and which she could not cradle in her arms like Reun.

Reun bent over and pressed her face against the baby's rosy cheeks. She was overcome with sadness. She lifted it up and held it a little distance away so she could have a good look at it. Her darling child. Its face was the image of its father's, from the eyebrows to the mouth and cheeks. Only the eyes were different. It had large, bright, innocent eyes, more gentle than the father's own bold eyes, which reflected his strength and resolve. She would be a comfort in times of difficulty. She was glad that it was a girl like herself. 'Don't struggle too much, little one. I'm not strong enough yet to stop you from falling out of my hands. I pray that you will grow up happy and contented. I've got the chance to see you, my darling. Not like your father. There's no hope that he will ever see whether this little face of yours is worthy of his own flesh and blood. Other people may say things and despise you for being born with no father, but I shall always be certain who your father is. You could only be your father's flesh and blood and he is a very respectable man. It's your karma to have a prostitute for a mother, a woman cursed and despised by everyone. If things had been different, I wouldn't have had to drag you around from one place to another, before you were even born. You would have had a father and relatives to look after you and play with you. Everything would have been perfect.'

But Reun kept all these thoughts to herself. Only her tears betrayed the terrible sadness she felt. The woman in the bed on her right looked at mother and child with womanly compassion.

'Oooh, isn't it sweet?' she could not help saying. 'Oh, it's crying. What a lot of noise!'

Reun turned and smiled in response to the woman's kindness, although her eyes were still full of tears. Awkwardly, like someone who had never done it before, she tried to soothe and quieten the baby. But just then, it stopped crying and gave up struggling in her arms of its own accord.

'The babe's father must be so pleased,' the woman said, smiling pleasantly and wanting to be friendly. She had no idea of the feelings that suddenly surged forth inside the infant's mother.

Reun looked up sadly, her face bathed in tears. 'The father's dead,' she replied, as she had determined she would. Then she began to cry quite uncontrollably once more. 'Oh, Good Lord!' There were gasps of sympathy. No wonder she had been crying as she cradled her child. 'Oh, isn't that tragic, never, ever seeing your own father?' one of the women added. 'And for her, too. Only a girl and a widow already.'

Reun made no reply. She just stared at her child's face. She gazed at it as if she were deep in thought. She did not really want to hand her child back to the nurse, who had come to collect it, but it was a hospital rule, and there was nothing she could do. Otherwise, she would have clung to it, and just sat admiring it. She gazed lovingly after it until the nurse had disappeared from sight. Then she lay down again, completely exhausted, with tears trickling silently down her face. She was on the point of dozing off, when she was startled by a loud noise next to her. She opened her eyes and looked over in the direction from where the noise was coming. It was the Chinese woman, crying when she saw her husband walking awkwardly towards her. The Chinese man's clothes were filthy. He was carrying things he had brought for his wife. He sat down opposite her, with reddened eyes, and they chatted noisily in Cantonese.

Reun closed her eyes. She did not want to look. Although the Chinese woman was very poor, she still had a husband to love and care for her, to bring things for her, and to sit and comfort her when she was down. She saw them talking things over together as a couple. The man was comforting his wife with gentle words, which she guessed were something like 'Don't be too upset about the baby. We're still alive and well and we can always try for another.' His wife's crying gradually grew quieter, until it stopped completely and gave way to the sound of chatter and giggling. Reun sighed heavily when she thought of her own loneliness, with no husband, like this Chinese woman had, to come and see her. She did not even have to see him. She just wanted to hear his voice. Then she would be overjoyed. But she still had no idea where Wit might be. My darling. You just left me, so heartlessly. You came and taught me the true meaning of love. Then you went and destroyed that love. Why did you say that you would try to find a way of getting some money so that you could marry me? Your wife's a filthy whore, not fit to go and live openly with you. Reun struggled to fight back the lump in her throat.

*   *   *

After Reun had been in hospital for five days, she began to miss Samorn. When she realized the pains were coming, she had immediately rushed to the hospital, without even telling Samorn. There were not many people around as kind as Samorn. And she probably would not come across her again in the next life. Whenever she got into difficulties, Samorn would always do her utmost to help, regardless of the inconvenience it might cause her. These thoughts had been crossing her mind, when by chance, that very day, Samorn came in to see her. She looked excited. Reun greeted her with a smile. She had been feeling lonely for several days, and unlike the other patients, she had not had a single visitor.

'Boy or a girl?' Samorn asked before she had even had time to sit down.

'A girl, 'Morn.'

'Oh no! What a pity. I wanted it to be a boy,' Samorn complained. 'How are things?' she asked, looking at Reun and seeing her cheerful expression. 'I was going to come and see you yesterday but I didn't get a chance.'

'I'm fine. Who told you where I was?'

'The day before yesterday, while I was out, I dropped in at Kesorn's house. She said you'd been in hospital several days. She's a bitch, that Kesorn,' Samorn added angrily. 'I'm sick of her.'

'What did she say?' Reun asked. Doubtless it was some-thing about her.

'What she said was, when you've had the baby, there's no need to go back there again and that it was a waste of money paying you, because you couldn't do anything apart from the washing, and that you were so slow. She went on and on like that.'

Tears welled up in Reun's eyes. She gave a deep, unhappy sigh. 'I don't know why it is I'm so unlucky,' she complained. 'Whoever I stay with, after just a short while, there's always someone who comes along and causes trouble.'

'Don't get worked up about it now,' said Samorn. 'Let me think a minute. I definitely don't want to stay at Ba Taht's, either. She's got someone new again. I don't know what she thinks is wrong with us. 'Win used to be the favourite, but she's out right now. Maybe I'll leave and rent a room. We could stay together. You could look after the baby and I could work when I needed. It's better than putting up with her foul mouth and her beating us whenever she feels like it.'

'It would be good if we could both stay together like you said. I wouldn't have to drag my child around from one place to another. Once you've got a child, it's not the same as when you're on your own.'

'Wait another two or three days and we should have some-thing sorted out. How many more days are you staying here?'

'It looks like the nurse said I've got to stay another ten days or something,' Reun replied. 'I'm not sure exactly. It's because I'm thin and I lost a lot of blood while I was giving birth. I've got to rest and get my strength back.'

'It's all right in here,' Samorn said, looking round. Wait until you're back to normal before you go home. If you come out now, you'll have nowhere to go. I'd really love to see the wee babe. What's it like? Does it look like its father?'

The words just slipped out of her mouth. She regretted them immediately. The blood raced to Reun's face, turning it a deep red, and then drained again, leaving her looking pale once more. She nodded sadly. Samorn knew how Reun must be feeling. 'You've got to stop being upset,' she urged. 'Just concentrate on looking after your child. Then you'll have someone to take care of you in your old age.'

'I don't expect gratitude or help from my child,' Reun replied softly. 'Don't look too far ahead, 'Morn. My own parents brought me up in the hope that they would have someone to depend on in their old age. Then I met someone better and just ran off after him and managed to lose everything in the process.'

Seeing that Reun was dragging up the past, Samorn quickly stopped her. 'Don't keep talking about what's in the past. It won't make things any better. It's better to try and think of the new place we're going to move to. There's good and bad in everyone's life, depending on their karma. People can't choose just the good things. If they could, no one would choose to be a prostitute. I'd be a *khunying* and you could be a *mom*, Reun.' She laughed softly as she steered the conversation towards a lighter vein so that Reun would forget her troubles for a while. Before she left, Samorn took about 2 baht in banknotes out of her purse and handed them to Reun. 'Here, take this and buy something to eat.'

With tears in her eyes, Reun gently pushed her hand away. 'Keep it, please,' she said. 'I've got enough. There are lots of other things you have to buy and then you go sharing them with me. I can't take it because I know very well that the only way you can make a living is....'

'Take it, Reun,' Samorn insisted, pressing the money into her hand. 'Do you think that if you really need it, you can just go and borrow it from anyone? Don't worry about me. When I run out, I can always pawn my skirt and blanket.'

Reun was choked with emotion. She sqeezed the hand of this woman who had shown her so much genuine kindness. 'I'm always troubling you, 'Morn. I've never done a single thing for you, and now you go and make me feel even more indebted. I feel awful about it.'

'Why do you always think that, Reun? I've already told you once before that I think of you as my sister. All I want is for us to be true friends. Let's just forget it. Whatever difficulties you face, I'll help you, even if it means I have to sell myself to do so.'

'No one has ever shown me so much love and concern as you, 'Morn. Wait until I come to live with you and then you will see just how much I love you, too.' Their eyes met. Even if they were not the eyes of pure, innocent young girls, there was a genuine purity and sincerity about them. They stood there, gazing deep into each other's soul, resolved to stand by each other, no matter what the future might hold. They talked about the new room for a while and Samorn promised she would return in two or three days' time with news of their new address.

*   *   *

On the prearranged day, Samorn returned, bringing with her various things for Reun and also some good news. She had found a place for them to rent. It was a single-storey shop-house on Worajak Road. It was not too cramped for the two of them, even with a baby. She had agreed to take it, paid in advance, and got them to clean it up. Tomorrow, she would fetch her things from Ba Taht's house, because she had sufficient money to settle all her debts. The day after tomorrow, Reun would be allowed to leave. Samorn would come and meet her and take her to their new home. Reun was overjoyed when she heard Samorn's news. She was pleased she would be free, with no one bossing her about, making her do this and that, and cursing her and making her life a misery. She was pleased, too, that she was going to live with Samorn, whom she both loved and admired.

During the course of the next day, however, Reun overheard something which touched a raw nerve inside her. It was said by some of the other women, further down, who were chatting. At first, Reun did not take much notice of who or what they were talking about. It was only when something caught her ear that she begun to take an interest.

'Oh, they were going at each other so much, the house nearly fell down,' said one of the women. 'No one dared stop them, because they're husband and wife and we're only relatives. If things had suddenly improved, where would that have left us?'

There was silence for a moment. Then another woman asked, 'And what happened to her fancy man, then?'

'Oh, he just disappeared into thin air. Then the husband chased his wife out of the house, child and all. There was a terrible scene. Chaos everywhere, and people crying their eyes out in the most heart-rending way.'

'Oh, so there was a child, too, then, was there? Good Lord. She certainly shouldn't have been messing around like that, then,' the other woman said indignantly.

'What do you mean, "she shouldn't have gone messing around like that"? Everyone knew all about her. Right from the start, we all tried to stop him, but he wouldn't listen. He went ahead and brought her in to stay with him. Now, before the child's a year old, there's trouble.'

'What's she like?' the other woman asked out of curiosity.

'She's a prostitute. What do you expect?' the first woman snapped.

Reun's heart missed a beat. She dared not look over in the women's direction. She lay there, stiffly, as if her very movements would betray her former occupation.

'Good heavens above!' her friend exclaimed in a shocked tone of voice. 'Hardly any wonder she was carrying on with some other fellow, then. But the father sounds like a strange fellow. What with plenty of girls around, he ignores them and goes and sets up with some prostitute. They say a leopard never changes its spots.'

'I'll tell you one thing. I can't stand even the sight of her. I don't want to go anywhere near her. And you won't catch me near her either,' she added. 'The moment she comes here, I go somewhere else. Filthy whore! Just meeting her makes you feel disgusted.'

Reun struggled to keep her silence. She was the kind of person who said exactly what she thought, and she almost got up, there and then, to announce, quite unashamedly, that the person lying beside them was just such a filthy, disgusting whore. But anxious to hear more, she made a great effort to control herself.

'It's a shame for the poor little child. Is it a girl or a boy?'

'A girl, and a bonny one at that. A pity the mother took it with her. When it grows up, it'll go just the same way as its mother, drifting around like that.'

'Right. It'll be just like its mother. If it'd been a boy, maybe things would be different.'

That was enough to make Reun think for several days. Her baby was a girl. She would have to take extra special care of her. At least it would have some of its father's blood. She did not want the child to turn out the way she had. It would be quite painful enough for the child, as it was, to be called the daughter of a prostitute. Back home, she had often heard her mother say, 'You can always tell an ox by its tail, and when it comes to a woman, you only have to look as far as her mother.' In other words, whatever the mother was like, the child would follow her example. And when she went to live with Samorn, who would be making a living in the same old way, her daughter would be growing closer to her, and growing like her, without her even realizing it. There was no way she wanted her daughter's life to be like her own, a life that people cursed and thought disgusting.

When the time came for the nurse to bring the baby back, Reun took the child and squeezed it tightly. 'My darling little girl,' she murmured, in a voice scarcely audible, 'I'll do everything to prevent this little bundle of flesh from becoming tarnished like its mother.'

Thirteen

THE small, rented room, which provided those three lives with a happy home, stood in a row of more than ten in Worajak Road. Although it was a little cramped, Reun and Samorn were pleased to be able to lead their own lives in their own modest way. It was better than living in a big house, having to depend on someone else for your food and having to put up with people cursing and mocking you whenever they felt like it.

When they first moved in, they were short of many household items and pieces of furniture. Reun found a curtain to divide the room into two, the outer part being for

Samorn to sleep in, while she and the baby had the inner. There was a low bench on which they put a mirror and powder bowls. Later, Reun urged Samorn to save up and get a cheap, wooden bed for Samorn herself to use. Now, a bed stood on the floor where Samorn used to sleep. Besides the bed, Samorn got a dressing-table and a wardrobe with a mirror from Werng Nakhorn Khasem. That was enough to make life comfortable.

Samorn acted as if she were the man of the house. Each night she went out to earn money in the same way she had since her days at Ba Taht's. It was a job forced on her by necessity. She could not just quit. She did not make very much. Just enough to live on and pay the rent without having to starve. During the daytime, if she did not have to go out, Samorn would help Reun to look after the baby. She tied the ends of a sarong to two posts and used it as a cradle. She would put the baby in and sing softly to it until it fell asleep. Some days Samorn went out and there was no one to rock the baby, so Reun would nurse it until it fell asleep and then put it down on the mattress. Then she would cover the child with a small mosquito net and go and do the washing and cleaning and sweep the room. Reun would not allow Samorn to lift a single finger to help with the housework. She looked after Samorn as a wife would a husband when he came home late, preparing food for her and keeping it so that the ants would not get at it.

One day, Samorn returned home to find Reun was not there. There was only the baby, lying among the dolls in front of the bed. Both doors were open and there was a trail of water from the front of the house right through to the back. She went out and looked up the road to the water pump and there she saw Reun on the way back with a can full of water. She stood there waiting until Reun had reached the front of the house and put the can down to rest. 'My

goodness, what are you fetching the water for?' she asked.
'You can pay the Chinese man to do it.'

'Why waste the money? The pump's right here and he
charges three satang for two trips. It's better to save the
money and buy *kanom*,' Reun added, as if the water cans she
had been carrying hardly weighed a thing.

'How much is it going to waste, then, for just two or three
people? If you go carrying heavy cans, you never know, you
might go and do yourself an injury. You've only just had a
baby and you're not over it, yet,' Samorn scolded, as she
watched Reun struggle to pour the water into the large
earthen jar on the kitchen veranda. Then she went off to find
the baby, picked her up, put her on her knee, and began to
tease her. Recognizing Samorn's face, the baby began to giggle
with pleasure. 'Now then,' she said to the baby, 'just you tell
Aunty if Mummy's naughty and goes out fetching water. She
needs a good smack, does your mum.' She looked closely at
the child's face and the shape of its mouth. The skin was soft
and fair and the bigger she got, the more like her father she
looked. It was almost as if they had come out of the same
mould, the only difference being that there was a manly
severity about the father's features. The only resemblance the
sweet little child bore to her mother was in her large round
eyes and long curly eyelashes. As Reun emerged smiling
from the inner room, Samorn turned and looked at the
mother's face. Reun was brighter and more cheerful than
before because she felt happy about where she was living and
she had a child to play with and hold and cuddle and keep
her company when things were bad. She was beginning to
look quite radiant.

Samorn was still unhappy about Reun working too hard.
'Don't go fetching any more water, Reun, believe me,' she
warned her. 'I don't like seeing you pounding away making
chilli paste for the curry. Isn't it tiring enough for you already?'

'What's the matter, 'Morn? All I'm doing is pounding chillies and fetching water. Back home, I've seen people working really hard and it doesn't seem to do them any harm. There, they start pounding the rice within a couple of months of giving birth. If they didn't, there wouldn't be any rice to eat.'

'So you want to go copying them, do you? People don't pound it themselves any more. They pay them at the rice mill to do it. Before, people used to do it themselves because there weren't any rice mills. You know, Reun,' Samorn continued critically, 'you've got one kid and you're still young, but you're letting yourself go. Just look at you. Your sarong is old and torn and it's been patched goodness knows how many times. I've bought you several new ones, but you keep them tucked away, as if they were too good to wear.'

What Samorn said was true. Reun was, indeed, still a fresh, young girl. But once she had begun to think of herself as a mother, she had let herself go. She no longer took care over her clothes and she let her hair grow long and unkempt, no longer bothering to put it up and arrange it tidily. Her face scarcely saw a speck of powder.

'It's perfectly all right to wear tatty old clothes at home,' Reun argued. 'I'm saving the new ones to wear when I go out,' she added, taking the child so she could feed it.

Samorn looked pitifully at the state of Reun. At Ba Taht's, all the other girls had helped Reun with clothes, so that even though she had just come from up-country, anyone seeing her would have said how nice she looked. Samorn herself had been overshadowed by her. But now, Reun hardly looked like her old self.

Samorn watched the child sucking milk in silence for a moment before she spoke. 'Can you make sure the room's nice and clean this evening, please? There's a man coming to see me here.'

Reun looked up in curiosity. 'Who is it, 'Morn?'

'He's got a wife and kids, but he wants a bit of fun on the side. He can only come and see me once a week, on a Saturday night. It doesn't matter, though. As things are, he said he'd give me 25 baht a month. We'll be all right then. Not bad, eh, Reun?'

Reun smiled happily at the news. ''Morn, that's really good about the extra income. You won't have to go out at night. You can stay at home with someone to take care of you and provide for you. And my child and I can depend on your kindness for support, too.' But at that moment, the smile on her face suddenly changed to a look of sadness.

'What is it now?' Samorn asked immediately, as she noticed the change in Reun's expression. 'One minute you're laughing, the next, you're white as a sheet.'

'Of course everyone likes money. But you're like my own sister. I don't want to see you among those women who offer their services for temporary pleasure....'

Samorn quickly covered Reun's mouth with her hand to prevent her from continuing. 'You're talking nonsense,' she said, forcing a laugh to conceal her sadness. 'Come on then, you sweet little thing. Come and see Aunty.' She took the child into her arms and held her up, but deep down she felt desperately sad.

*   *   *

Some people think that those woman who are labelled prostitutes have no problems at all. They dress themselves up in attractive clothes and earn their money in an easy way. But little do such people know what sadness lies beneath those faces which have been made up to please others. They are condemned to being playthings, providing pleasure for others, while they themselves are denied happiness and are despised.

*   *   *

That night Samorn did not have to go out as usual. She received her generous visitor at home with Reun's full co-operation. He left early on Sunday morning. This continued every Saturday, and at the end of the month, he gave Samorn 25 baht. This they used to pay the rent, buy rice, and settle various other expenses, including their day-to-day food, without Samorn having to go out on her own at night to earn extra. Life was gradually becoming reasonably pleasant and relaxing.

After about three months, the man's visits became less frequent. At first he came every other Saturday. But after a while, he just disappeared altogether. When he stopped coming, Samorn's monthly income came to an end. But it did not upset her unduly. She understood such things. The only thing that did depress her a little was that the time had come for her to go out and work again, as she had before. Reun, too, was unhappy about this, and from time to time she would complain about him disappearing.

'Don't go moaning about him, Reun. He's a man. He's not going to be content with just one woman. When he comes across anyone he fancies, he'll be off after her, looking for a bit of fun for a while. You can't expect very much from them. Besides, I certainly didn't love him. It was just a matter of doing my job, a way of bringing in the money for us to live on. If he doesn't come, I can just put my head down and get back to working. If a fish will keep on wriggling until its scales have dried up, what have I got to be afraid of?' she added casually.

*   *   *

Samorn went back to her old work. She worked hard, some days bringing in a lot of money, others only a little. She neither slept nor rested as she had before. Her physical appearance began to deteriorate visibly. Reun begged her to rest a little, but she refused. She could not stop, because if she did, it would mean hardship for her, for Reun, and for her bright-eyed little niece. She had to struggle on until she got some money.

It was dusk, one day, and Samorn had gone out. Reun began to nurse her child to sleep. The baby had missed her daytime nap because she had been busy playing with a doll that her aunt had bought for her. When evening came, the child was tired and fretful, and it was nearly nine o'clock before Reun got her off to sleep. Carefully, she sat up and tucked the baby up in a blanket. Gazing at the child lying there asleep, her mind went back to the time when she had Wit lying by her side. She had extracted herself from his embrace and then stolen a careful look at his face, just as she was now looking at her child. She had gently rubbed her nose against his cheek to wake him, just like a mother gently kisses her sleeping child, fearful lest it wake. A mosquito buzzed close to her ear. If she ignored it, it would bite her child. She struck a match and lit the candle which she had put in the nappy bowl. She began to look for it, but without success. She returned to the baby. It gave a tiny cry as the large mosquito withdrew its long pointed mouth from her reddened cheek. The blood which it had sucked from the baby was clearly visible in its transparent belly. She would wait until the baby had gone back to sleep and then she would put an end to it. She followed it closely as it flew over and settled on the mosquito net. In one hand she held the candle. With the other, she patted her daughter, singing softly to her until the child went back to sleep. Then she turned round and held the candle flame up against the mosquito's body. It fell down on to the mattress. She shone the light all around but she could not see any others. Then she blew the candle out and emerged from the mosquito net.

After brushing down Samorn's mattress and making sure there was no dust on it to irritate her, Reun went and stood outside at the front of their house. The sky was overcast, as if it were going to rain, and the wind was stronger than usual. Someone came by selling sweets and desserts, and she stopped the vendor to buy *kloo-ay boo-ut chee*. She put them in a little bowl and placed the bowl in another bowl of water, ready for Samorn. Then she prepared water for bathing just as it began to drizzle. There was a flash of lightning and a terrifying crack of thunder.

Reun was unable to sleep. She was worried about Samorn and afraid that she would get caught in the rain. She tossed and turned restlessly. Outside came the sound of footsteps. Thinking it was Samorn returning, she got out of the mosquito net and rushed to open the door for her. But it was the person who lived opposite, coming back from the cinema. Reun sighed deeply and prayed that it would stop raining. Cold and shivering, she went back to bed and slept fitfully until two o'clock, when she heard a loud knocking on the door and Samorn's voice calling out to her above the noise of pounding rain to come and open the door. Reun rushed to undo the lock and Samorn pushed her way in, soaked to the skin, her teeth chattering with the cold. Reun helped her off with her wet things.

'Is there anything to eat?' Samorn asked in a shaking voice as she changed her clothes. 'I'm really starving—and freezing.'

'There's *kloo-ay boo-ut chee*,' Reun replied, bringing out the bowl. She fetched the lamp, which was standing against the wall, and put it down near the bowl.

'Is there anything else apart from *kloo-ay boo-ut chee*? I could do with something more filling.'

'No, there's nothing at all. I didn't think you'd want anything, so I didn't get anything,' Reun replied and hurried into the kitchen. She took out a bowl and began to rummage for some coins. A moment later she walked past Samorn, who was drying her hair on a towel.

'Where are you going, Reun? No. No, don't, there's no need,' Samorn protested. 'It's pouring. The *kloo-ay boo-ut chee* will do fine. All the shops are closed now.'

Reun ignored her protests. 'The shop on the corner is open all night,' she replied, and rushed out before Samorn could call her back.

Reun ran out into the pouring rain and returned with *kao tom pla* for Samorn. Samorn ate quickly as she was so hungry, scarcely pausing for breath and not raising her head until the bowl was empty. After the small bowl of *kloo-ay boo-ut chee* and a cup of water, she felt better and less tired, for she had seen Reun's concern. It was not a wasted effort to love Reun as if she were her own sister. Indeed, if it had not been for Reun running out to buy her food, Samorn felt sure that she would have fainted at some point during the last five minutes.

The next morning Samorn did not feel very well. She felt weak and had a slight pain in the back of her head. She thought it must be because she had been hungry and exhausted and had got soaked the previous night, but she did not mention it to Reun. When evening came, she simply got dressed and went out as usual.

Two or three days later, Reun noticed that Samorn was looking distinctly pale, and had been coughing a bit during the night. When evening came and Samorn was getting ready, Reun protested. 'You look so pale, 'Morn. Don't go. Give it a miss for one night.'

'What do you mean, "pale"?' Samorn replied, forcing a laugh and standing up close to Reun for her to see. 'I can't, anyway. I've got a date tonight.'

Reun gave a long, unhappy sigh. Watching Samorn get dressed, she saw how much paler she was than before and how sunken her eyes looked, like someone whose strength had all been drained. 'Last night you were coughing all night long,' Reun remarked, unable to stop herself.

'So? Coughing's no big deal, is it?' Samorn said, looking at herself in the mirror. She was shocked by what she saw. She was so pale there was no sign of blood. Before leaving the house, she powdered her face to conceal her pallor, and applied lipstick to make herself look more attractive.

Sadly, Reun watched her, until she disappeared from sight. Samorn was putting up with all the hardship and exhaustion for her and her child. The next night she went out again, but her condition had worsened; as she had only a slight fever, she put up with it. She returned quite early that night. Reun went to the door to greet her. 'You're back early tonight,' she said. 'Don't you feel well?'

Samorn nodded, unable to conceal her condition any longer. 'I went to the doctor's.... Oh! No! I didn't go to the doctor's at all,' she said, instantly denying her slip of the tongue. Her eyes were red with fever. Reun stood there amazed by Samorn's confused reply. She touched Samorn on the top of her arm. It was like fire.

'My goodness! You're so hot. You'd better get to bed right away.'

Utterly exhausted, Samorn did as she was told. She lay down on the pillow and remained silent. As Reun ran her hand across her forehead, she grabbed it and clasped it tightly in her own icy hands. She opened her eyes which were heavy with fever and looked at Reun. 'I've got to try and earn some money,' she said hoarsely. 'We've hardly got any left.'

'Never mind that now. You've still got me. Just get some sleep and maybe you'll be better tomorrow.' Reun covered her with a blanket and then left her mosquito net and went back to her own and lay down next to the baby. She could scarcely sleep for fear that Samorn might be unwell during the night and that she might not hear if she called. It was almost three o'clock in the morning before she finally dozed off.

Fourteen

REUN was woken by a tiny, soft hand, tugging at her nose. She opened her eyes to find the baby sprawled alongside her and calling her in throaty gurgles. Every morning, when it was still dark, she would lift the child up and then lovingly place it on top of herself. She would tease her and they would laugh and play together like any mother and child. But this morning was different. Reun got up quickly and carried the baby over to Samorn's bed. She opened the mosquito net. 'How do you feel, 'Morn?' she asked.

Samorn moved slightly. 'The headache's got worse,' she said. She sounded feverish. 'Reun, can you go and get me a pill for the fever. You can leave the little one here,' she added, gently patting the bed beside her, as if all the energy had been drained from her.

'She'll disturb you,' said Reun. 'I can't leave her with you. I'll take her with me.' Without pausing to wash her face, she took the money Samorn had given her the previous day from the cardboard box and went out to get the pills that would make Samorn better.

Three days passed and Samorn's condition had still not improved. Every day she had had a headache and had been shivering with cold. Now, in addition, she had developed a persistent cough. She had to lie down quietly. Reun dashed about, looking after the baby and acting as nurse, all on her own. She would not sleep. Some nights she stayed up keeping an eye on Samorn until daylight. Poverty made it impossible for her to bring a doctor to treat Samorn. Apart from taking pills for the fever and aspirins, quinine, and *ya hom*, it was difficult to know what to do.

As Samorn had not been out working for several nights because of her illness, the small amount of money they had inevitably diminished. Reun felt more and more depressed. The three or four pills she had bought were gone now. She went into the kitchen to boil some rice for Samorn. She picked up a match, lit the ashes, and bent down to scoop up some charcoal from the wooden crate. There was only a little left. She carried the pot over to the rice bucket and lifted the corrugated iron lid off. There was only one canful left. Tomorrow there would hardly be enough to eat. Reun felt more and more dispirited. Who would lend them any money?

When the *kao tom* was ready, she grilled a dried fish and then pounded it into small pieces, which she put in the bowl and took over to Samorn, who lay there drowsily, her face pale, her eyes vacant and her lips dry.

'Try to force yourself to eat some *kao tom*,' Reun begged her. 'Just two or three spoonfuls, all right? It's still warm.'

Samorn shook her head. 'Water ... water,' she cried in a hoarse voice. 'All I want is water.'

'Wouldn't it be better if you took some *kao tom*?' Reun asked with concern. 'You haven't eaten a thing. All you've had for two days is water. Just try and take a few spoonfuls.'

'I don't want anything to eat,' Samorn replied wearily.

'No one wants to eat when they're sick, 'Morn. You've got to force yourself. Even just the soup from the *kao tom* would do you good. It would be enough to fill your stomach up a bit so you don't start fainting again,' Reun added encouragingly. 'All right then? I'll feed you.'

When Samorn saw that Reun was going to make her eat, she raised her head and opened her mouth to take the *kao tom*. She turned it over in her mouth slowly, really having to force herself as Reun had said. After three spoonfuls, Samorn shook her head and refused the fourth. Reun put down the bowl and brought some water for her to rinse her mouth and drink. Before Reun had time to wash the bowl, she heard the door open and caught sight of the rent-collector. She realized that Samorn had put off paying until today. Her expression immediately turned to one of gloom.

'So what's up with you, then, 'Morn,' the middle-aged woman who collected the rent for the owner of the shop-houses greeted her when she saw Samorn lying in bed, covered with a blanket like an invalid.

Reun rushed out to intercept her. ''Morn isn't very well,' she said, before Samorn had a chance to reply. 'She went down with a fever several days ago. Would you like to sit down?' Reun fetched a glass of water and set it down in the middle of the room. 'Please sit over on the mat. It's dirty just there.'

'Don't worry. Just here will do nicely. Everyone seems to be going down with a fever at the moment,' the woman said, fingering the fold of her sarong. She took out a piece of paper and began to unfold it before handing it to Reun. 'I've come for the rent,' she continued. 'Last time 'Morn asked to put off payment until today. Here you are. Here's the receipt. You've had almost half a month.'

When Reun made no attempt to take the receipt but just sat there in silence, the rent-collector knew immediately that something was wrong.

'What's the matter? Why haven't you got the money for me? The rent is only 7 baht a month.'

'I'm ... I'm going to have to ask if we can postpone paying for a bit longer,' Reun said, the words slipping pathetically from her mouth. She heard Samorn move awkwardly on the bed and felt uneasy. She did not want Samorn to have to start worrying about this.

With a look of displeasure, the woman turned and spoke to Samorn rather than Reun. 'What's all this, then, 'Morn? Didn't you tell me you'd pay me today?'

Alarmed, Reun tried to stop her. ''Morn isn't at all well. Please don't go talking to her. I've already asked you if we can put it off again. Surely you could wait a bit and collect two months together.'

'You've already put it off once and now you're wanting to put it off again,' the woman said. 'I come along one day to collect the rent and you want me to come back the next. You're not going to give me the rent for just one month, then you want me to collect for two months together. Nowhere else is it as difficult to collect the rent as it is here.' She stuffed the receipt back into the fold of her sarong and her expression hardened as she glanced contemptuously at the two girls. 'So in the end I have to pay my tram fare here all for nothing. It seems funny to me why, if you haven't got the money to pay the rent, you don't just go and live in a brothel, once and for all.' She spoke bluntly with chilling words.

People might put up with contempt from a benefactor, but this was just a servant who had been sent to collect the money by her boss. It was not right that she should start getting so aggressive. Samorn, who was by nature hot-tempered, leapt out of bed, forgetting that she was sick and made straight for the woman. 'Now just you watch what you say,' she yelled, 'or I'll have you down at the police station.'

The woman balked and fled towards the corner of the room, staring in terror at Samorn's raised arm, for it looked as if Samorn really was going to hit her. Reun was about to scream in alarm for she knew all too well about Samorn's violent temper. Once she had even sent Tawin crashing down the stairs. But now, she really was not well. Reun was afraid that if she did not stop her, something nasty might happen. Besides, Samorn's condition had worsened.

Reun quickly grabbed Samorn by the wrist and held her. 'Don't, 'Morn, you're not well. Come and lie down.' Reun led her over towards the bed, but Samorn was not going quietly. Gasping for breath and with a wild look in her eyes, she stared straight at the heartless rent-collector.

'You're just a servant. Your boss makes you come and collect the rent and that's all. So why do you have to come here cursing and swearing at us? I'm a prostitute and going to the police station doesn't bother me.'

'So who was it then who had me come and collect it today?' the woman demanded, her face reddening. 'Do you know how many times I've had to pay the tram fare back and forth? Wouldn't it make you just a little bit angry?'

'I've always been reliable before,' Samorn said. 'It's only this month and that's because I'm sick. I don't know where I'm going to get the money from in time so that's why I've got to ask for another postponement.' As she finished speaking, she collapsed on to the bed. Reun looked at her anxiously.

'What I'm afraid is that if I come round for it another day I still won't get it,' the woman said, turning away. She stormed out of the room, half afraid that if she lingered she would be hauled off to the police station by Samorn and beaten up into the bargain.

'Oh dear,' said Reun. 'You shouldn't have got angry and got up, you know. You've been a bit better today. You've managed to eat some fish and rice.'

Samorn sighed with misery. 'How could anyone put up with someone like that cursing them? I felt like giving her a good slap in the face.'

'If you were well, it would've been different,' said Reun. 'But you really are ill. Look at you, when you just get up and go that far.' She found the *ya hom* and dissolved it in warm water for Samorn. Here, take this quickly or you'll really be feeling worse.'

Samorn swallowed the medicine and then told Reun to fetch her purse from the wardrobe. 'Have a look inside. There should be some money there.'

As she opened the purse, Reun felt relieved to think that Samorn must have more money put aside. But she was wrong. Her face turned pale when all she found were a few satang coins amounting to only 80 satang or so. She was silent until Samorn asked how much there was.

'Three baht,' Reun lied, wanting to ease Samorn's worries.

Samorn frowned and then met Reun's eyes. She tried to smile to show she knew what Reun was up to, but she was not well enough to manage it. 'What do you mean, 3 baht? I remember breaking into my last baht when I paid the rickshaw boy 20 satang. Don't go trying to fool me, Reun,' she added sadly in a low voice. 'We've hardly got any money left, you know. Never mind, though. I might be better today or tomorrow. Maybe I'll be able to go out and earn a little bit.'

'You mustn't,' Reun quickly forbade her. 'You're not better yet. Just leave things to me.'

All day long, Reun wondered where she would get the money for them to live on and to buy Samorn's medicine once their last 80 satang were gone. Was she going to stand by so heartlessly and watch while Samorn, who had shown her such kindness, forced herself out to earn some money in spite of her illness, so as to look after Reun and her baby? Where was she going to get any money from? Such thoughts left her feeling utterly helpless and despondent. She looked down at the necklace which Wit had placed around her neck with his own hands on the last day he had come to see her. The thought that it was worth enough to be able to exchange for the money they needed to support them broke her heart. She had never taken it off since the day Wit had placed it round her neck. She intended to keep it and pass it on to her daughter as a reminder of Wit, who had now dis-appeared from her life and whom she no longer had any hope of ever meeting again. To repay Samorn's kindness and support herself, Reun was prepared to pawn it. But she would not get very much and when it was all gone she would have to look for more.

There was only one alternative. The thought of it sent a cold chill right through her heart. It was the easiest way to earn money and she had done it before. Reun had already made up her mind that, for her daughter's sake, she would under no circumstances place herself in a position where she would be scorned and despised by others. She felt a sense of revulsion at the thought of returning to her old profession. The more she thought about it, the more agitated and unhappy she became.

As dusk fell, Samorn's condition worsened once more. She had a temperature, her lips were dry, and she slept fit-fully. As she lay there delirious, Reun stood watching, tears streaming down her cheeks. Samorn had been so good to her. No matter how little she had, she had helped willingly, rushing around trying to find a place for Reun and to make things easier for her. But now, with Samorn lying there sick, Reun was doing nothing to help her get better except just standing and watching, waiting for death which was creeping nearer with every terrifying moan that passed Samorn's lips. Reun felt sick at heart. Everywhere people called her a pros-titute. Let them label her like that for the rest of her life. There was no longer any point in saving herself for someone. He must have forgotten her by now. There was no one to see her hardship and suffering. In that instant, her mind was made up, once and for all. Her face was strained and tears welled up in her eyes.

Reun picked up the last remaining pill and dissolved it in a glass of water, and then, holding Samorn's mouth open, she poured the mixture down. She coaxed the baby to sleep quickly, blocking everything out of her mind. She hardly even wanted to look at her little daughter's face. She took off the necklace that Wit had given her and placed it round the sleeping infant's neck. Then she got up and went outside to have a bath and get dressed. She chose some decent clothes from her days at Ba Taht's. They were already ironed and still reasonably fashionable. It was a long time since she had dressed up nicely like this. She powdered her face, combed out the long untidy strands of hair, and rubbed hair oil in before tying it up in a small bun. She took Samorn's lipstick and smeared her lips a light red. With her face made up like this and her jet-black eyes, who would have guessed that she was the mother of a seven-month-old child? When she was ready, she turned the lamp down a little lower and left the room quickly, not daring to go too near her daughter's mosquito net.

The mixture which Reun had poured down Samorn's throat began to take effect reducing her fever during the course of the night. This, together with the sound of her niece crying unusually loudly, made Samorn wake with a start, bathed in sweat. Why didn't she hear Reun comforting the child as she usually did? The only sound came from the child crying and it was getting louder and louder. She called out, but heard no answer. Alarmed, she quickly got out of bed and, forgetting her fever, pulled the mosquito net open. There was no sign of Reun. What was this? Where had Reun gone at this late hour? She called out twice more but there was still no response. With a great effort, she picked the baby up, freed it from its soaking nappy and changed it into a new one. As she soothed the child, she was wondering all the time what had happened to Reun. The shock seemed to have completely cured her fever. When the baby had gone back to sleep, she emerged from the mosquito net, still not completely sure that Reun was not around. She held up the lamp and shone it into the kitchen, but there was no sign of her. As she came back out, she almost dropped the lamp in surprise. Reun had come in through the door and was standing there quietly. In the light Samorn saw a figure wearing an old dress that she remembered from the days at Ba Taht's. Sorrow and regret lay concealed behind the pale face.

'Reun!' cried Samorn in a single word of greeting.

'Yes, it's me,' Reun replied in a normal voice, even smiling brightly as if there was nothing unusual about her. 'What did you get up for?'

'Where on earth have you been at this time of night?' Samorn asked, unable to contain her curiosity. Her sunken eyes fixed on the other girl's face as if searching out the truth. 'The baby was crying and I had to get up to have a look. I was only just going back to bed now.'

'Oh, she was crying, was she?' Reun asked, glancing quickly over in the direction of the mosquito net. 'Here, let me have it,' she said, taking the lamp from Samorn, 'and you get back to bed.'

'First, tell me where you've been, Reun,' Samorn pleaded, placing a feverish hand on Reun's arm.

Reun smiled cheerfully. 'Let's talk tomorrow. You go to bed now, and I'll go and have a bath.' Without waiting for Samorn to question her further, Reun walked out round the back leaving Samorn to force herself back inside her mosquito net, without having got a single thing out of Reun.

When Reun got into her mosquito net, the baby was fast asleep, its eyes tightly closed and two hands stretched out on the bed. The cheerful face that Samorn had seen a moment ago had turned pale and tears now trickled down the cheeks. Reun dared not cry aloud for fear that Samorn would hear.

For a long time, she just sat there motionless. Eventually, she buried her head down beside the baby's mattress in utter misery.

Fifteen

THE next day Samorn's condition had improved sufficiently for her to be able to get up from the bed where she had lain delirious for several days and go and play with the baby. She was waiting for an opportunity to ask Reun about the curious events of the previous night. But now was not the time.

Reun went out again that morning but soon returned. Apart from the grilled bananas and a packet of tablets that she had brought with her, she also had a Chinese man following along behind with a sack of rice on his back. Where had Reun been last night? And where had she got the money to buy these things from? Samorn wondered. She became even more curious when she heard Reun summoning the Chinese charcoal-seller. She waited while Reun finished sweeping the house and then came over to sit near her while she fed the baby. She had been bursting with curiosity from the moment she had woken up. 'Last night?' she asked. 'Last night ...?'

Reun seemed to understand the question and to have been expecting it. 'Oh, you mean last night,' she replied immediately, 'when the baby was crying? It was probably because its nappy was soaking or something. It's really funny. Other people's babies aren't like that at all. Up-country mothers have to go out working in the fields, planting and harvesting rice. They leave the children in a cot where they get wet and dirty, yet you never see anyone's child crying, not even a little bit. They just sleep through it all. Sometimes they just put them down on the ground out in the open and

leave them crawling and playing around and nothing happens
to them. You never see anyone come to any harm or get sick.
But the ones that are really carefully looked after are the ones
that are always getting ill.'

Reun spoke so quickly that it was impossible to interrupt,
and from the look on her face, she seemed to be quite carried
away by what she was saying. Samorn took a deep breath and
broke in. 'No, what I meant was....'

'Oh, you mean the dress I was wearing last night? It was
the one we went to Pahurat together to buy the material for
and which I had made up at that shop in front of the house. I
can still wear it. It doesn't look too bad.'

Samorn's patience snapped. She waved her hand in irritation to stop Reun from carrying on any further. 'Where did
you go last night, Reun?' she asked, bringing her face up
close to Reun's. 'And what's more,' she gasped, scarcely able
to draw her breath, 'where did you get the money for the
food and charcoal from?'

Reun lowered her head and remained silent. She pretended to be watching her child with its eyes open, contentedly sucking milk on her lap. She tried to avoid the
painful question, but there was no way out. As she looked up
slowly, Samorn could see the tears in her dark, innocent eyes.

'You know very well what chance I've got of earning any
money apart from....' She fought back the choking sensation
in the back of her throat. 'Apart from going back to the old
days and what I used to do.'

'Reun!' cried Samorn, shocked.

'Yes, 'Morn, I have to go back to that wretched life
because I can't bear to see you suffer. You've been so good to
me. Just like a mother, a real mother, who never lets her child
suffer any hardships. Ever since we were at Ba Taht's house,
you've gone out of your way to help me and make me happy.
It was you who advised me to run away to Khun Luang's

house and then when I went to Kesorn's house, you didn't abandon me. You've continued to support and feed both me and my child, and now, when you are ill, and we scarcely have anything to eat and no medicine, I can't just sit back and watch someone who has been so kind to me suffer scorn and hardship. So I must go out to earn some money.' She spoke in a trembling voice and the tears that had been welling up in her eyes began to stream down her cheeks.

Samorn was silent. She did not cry like Reun, but inside, her heart swelled with emotion. It was some time before she spoke. 'I don't want you to go sacrificing yourself to that kind of life for my sake,' she said in a husky voice.

'It's not just for you,' Reun countered. 'It's for the baby, too. I realize that, no matter what, I'm going to have to struggle to get the money to look after my child until she is grown up. I can't just leave her and forget about her, like some people do, because a child is too innocent to have to bear the sins of its parents. If we bring one into the world, we must give it love and support until the day we die.'

Samorn felt some relief when she realized that Reun was not doing it just for her sake but also for that of the little child. 'What are you going to do about the baby?' she asked. 'Who's going to look after it? I don't feel at all happy about what you're doing.'

'There's no problem,' Reun replied. 'Today I'm going to have a word with Mae Peu-ut from opposite, to see if I can pay her to look after the babe. She might agree because she hasn't got any children of her own.'

'You mean *that* Mae Peu-ut?' Samorn said. 'I don't really trust her. I don't know what kind of a person she is.'

'She can't be that bad. Besides, she looks as if she's fond of kids, too. She often comes and plays with the baby on the quiet.'

Samorn gave a deep sigh. 'Even so, I still don't like the idea. I don't like you going back to that kind of a life. Just look at me. You don't have to tell me anything about being looked down on. It only gets worse. The older you get, the less attractive you become. It's a real drag. There's never enough money, and it's no longer as easy to bring it in as it once was. There's another thing. You're still too young and too straight and honest to understand men properly. In this kind of life and this line of work, the word 'love' is meaningless. There's only want. You have to know enough not to be taken in by them when they say things like 'I love you'. We love them because it's our job and we have to. Just look at Khun Nop, that fellow who used to come and see me every Saturday.'

'Mmm, yes, you're right,' cried Reun, remembering the man. 'Now he doesn't come any more.'

'Exactly. And goodness only knows how many times he must have told me he loved me and cared for me. I listened to him, but I didn't love him in return because I knew perfectly well what this kind of man's love meant. Even when he didn't come again, I didn't miss him or give him any more thought. It's happened to me so many times. In this kind of life, sometimes you even have to teach them.'

'Teach who?' Reun asked with curiosity.

'Young men. Some young fellows see me walking about by myself and try to chat me up without realizing they're heading for danger. Some of them even go as far as stealing money from their parents to give to me. I give it back and tell them not to go falling in love with me, that people like me aren't fit for love.'

Samorn saw Reun heave a deep sigh. 'That's the way things are, though,' she added. 'I'd like you to find a nice man and settle down properly so that you can provide security for your child. Don't go hanging around for Khun Wit. He may have forgotten you by now, for all I know.'

'No, I'm not waiting for him any more. Even if I met him, I wouldn't want anything from him, except just to tell him about the baby. Maybe it would be good for the child if he believed it was his.'

'I've never ever had such hope, nor shall I,' Samorn murmured.

*   *   *

That afternoon Reun agreed to pay the neighbour, Mae Peu-ut, Nai Klin's wife, to look after her child. In fact, Mae Peu-ut did not particularly like Samorn and Reun, even though both were kind and had done nothing to upset relations with the neighbours. The reason she disliked and despised them was because Samorn was, as they say, 'on the game'. But if someone was going to give her money or there was some benefit to be gained, Mae Peu-ut would do it. She agreed somewhat half-heartedly, on the grounds that 5 baht was not enough, what with having to worry about boiling water, boiling milk, and then having to lose sleep at night, too. Reun did not want to argue about money; if she did, Mae Peu-ut would surely accept her terms, but then later, she might not take proper care of the child. So, for the sake of the child's safety, Reun agreed to pay 6 baht a month. The cost of tinned milk was extra and Mae Peu-ut would ask for this at regular intervals.

For the first two days Reun would not risk stopping breastfeeding altogether and putting the baby straight on to tinned milk, so she breastfed during the day and gave tinned milk at night. In the evenings, she sadly carried the child over to Mae Peu-ut's. If it were not out of necessity, she would never let her child out of her arms; but because she was poor, she had to struggle to support her with her own efforts.

Mae Peu-ut and Nai Klin came out and greeted her heartily. 'Don't worry about anything,' Nai Klin said. 'I'll look after her as if she were my own. Peu-ut and I haven't any of our own. Just tell me what brand of milk you give her so that I can get the right one.'

Reun gave him 2 baht for the tinned milk. "Morn and I thought we'd give her "Bear Brand".'

'Good gracious, that's rather extravagant, isn't it?' said Mae Peu-ut as she took the money and counted it out. 'It's over 40 satang a tin. This 2 baht must be for the milk. Right, in a moment I'll pop out and buy a bottle and teat for the milk so that I can use it tonight.'

'Yes, I'll give you this 2 baht first and when that's gone, I'll give you some more. It may be extravagant, but what else can I do? It's true, there are other kinds of milk which are cheaper, but you can't be too sure of them. When you get the milk ready, could you make sure the water is boiling, please,' Reun stressed anxiously as she looked sadly at the child in her arms.

'Huh! You talk as if I were an idiot,' Mae Peu-ut cried.

'No, that's not what I meant,' said Reun in hurried denial. 'If I did think that, I wouldn't let you look after her.'

The look of displeasure gradually faded from Mae Peu-ut's face. Nai Klin held out his arms to the baby and called to it in encouragement. 'Come on then, old girl, come and see Uncle. Have you given her a name yet, Reun?'

"Morn and I haven't decided on a name yet, so we're call-ing her 'Eet' for now,' Reun replied. 'Off you go then,' she said, handing the baby over into his outstretched arms, 'go and see Uncle.'

Even though the baby was only just over six months old, it could clearly see the unfamiliar face of the person holding it. Eet struggled and cried for her mother. Reun lowered her head and a tear trickled from her eye. Just then her gaze alighted upon her beloved's necklace which she had placed around the child's neck and this made her feel even more upset. Unable to bear sitting there any longer, she rose and returned to her house, ignoring the cries of her child. There, she slumped down crying beside Samorn, who lay in bed, her own eyes misted with tears from the moment she had seen Reun rushing into the room.

At dusk, seeing Samorn's condition slightly improved, Reun went out, because she did not want the sound of Eet's cries echoing in her ears. It was dark before she returned and Mae Peu-ut's door was closed. She listened intently, but could hear no sound of her daughter fretting. It was daylight before she managed to get to sleep; she could not help worrying that Mae Peu-ut would not be capable of looking after Eet the way she wanted her to. It was boiling the water for the milk that she was most concerned about. It wasn't just that it would cause ordinary diarrhoea if Mae Peu-ut was careless about making sure that it was boiled first; diarrhoea could develop into something else more serious. Furthermore, when she went to bed, Mae Peu-ut would think only of her own comfort. She would not be listening for the hum of mosquitoes, and even if she did hear any, she would think that just one would not be able to suck out very much blood. She would probably let it take its fill of blood from her little baby, her darling little child who would scream because of the bite and would not be easily calmed because the voice trying to offer her comfort would not be the voice of the mother she was used to. And when the child would not calm down, Mae Peu-ut would get annoyed and start pinching her on the arms and legs as Reun had seen some women do to their children. Her child would be covered in terrible dark bruises.

If her darling child could feel as its mother did now, how hurt would it feel that its mother was abandoning it to the care of someone else, instead of looking after it herself? It could blame her for bringing a child into the world without offering it any of the happiness other mothers give their children. She accepted this fate, a fate born of thoughtless action and lack of foresight. She alone accepted it, the child's father sharing no part in it, for he did not know, had absolutely no idea, that somewhere he had a child in need of his care and protection.

Two or three days later, Eet really was ill. When Reun took her to the clinic, she learned that it was as a result of changing over to tinned milk; the child's stomach was not yet accustomed to this kind of food. After taking the medicine from the clinic, Eet was soon back to normal and her fretfulness disappeared. Gradually, she became quite used to the couple; but she was not distant with her mother. Reun came to play with her every day as a matter of routine and some days would take her to see Samorn, who was, little by little, recovering from her sickness.

Mae Peu-ut and Nai Klin at first did all they could to gain Reun's trust. In the morning when Eet woke up, Mae Peu-ut bathed her. She soaped her all over, washing her down with warm water until she was nice and clean and then dried her and rubbed talcum powder on her. She gave her a bottle of warm cow's milk to drink every three hours, as the nurse had advised, and then let her sleep for a while. She gave the child her care and devotion as if it really were her own. One day, Reun had nothing to do. She had already prepared the rice and fish for Samorn and was thinking about her child. Like any other mother, she wanted to play with her child, especially now that Eet was beginning to babble away once she was propped up. She was becoming even cuter.

Reun walked quietly into Mae Peu-ut's home without Mae Peu-ut realizing, as she was busy in the kitchen, preparing the evening meal. Eet was lying stretched out on the wooden floor, happily playing with a puddle of water. Reun picked up her child, automatically glancing over towards the wall as she did so. What caught her maternal eye was another tin of cow's milk. It was a poor-quality brand which they sold in the market. The lid was off and there were dirty milk stains down the side. It was standing in a plate half-filled with water, and there beside it, was Eet's bottle of milk. Was it possible that Mae Peu-ut would deceive her? That she would take the money for 40-satang tins and then go and buy ones costing 13 or 14 satang instead? Before Reun's doubts could grow any deeper, Mae Peu-ut hurried out from the kitchen.

'Oh, Reun, it's you. I was inside, getting some food. Oh dear! You've knocked the water over, then, have you, my little darling? Dear, oh dear!' she said, laughing good-humouredly. 'Do you see, the cup of water was over there and she's gone and pulled it over and tipped it all over her tummy. What a mess!' But when she caught sight of the can of milk which she had absent-mindedly left out, her expression immediately changed. She did not know whether Reun had seen it or not. She sat down in such a way as to block Reun's view and asked, 'How's 'Morn? Much better now, is she?'

'Yes, much better now,' replied Reun. 'Another two or three days and I should think she'll be back to normal.' Mae Peu-ut's manner banished any doubts Reun might have had. She did not want to think that someone was not being straight with her, because apart from the unhappiness it would cause her, it would also increase her feelings of an-imosity towards that person. She chatted away in a neigh-bourly manner as she played with the child and forgot all about the can of poor-quality milk until the evening when she left. But before leaving the house, she glanced over to where the tin of milk had been. It was not there. It had disap-peared. Immediately, all Reun's doubts returned. Where had the can of milk gone? If Mae Peu-ut had moved it somewhere else when she was chatting with her, then she had done so without turning round and drawing any attention at all to the tin. Reun walked back preoccupied to where Samorn was sitting. She could not stop herself from telling Samorn all her doubts about the milk.

'It's best to pretend you don't know what's going on,' Samorn murmured after a while. 'Just think of the child's happiness. Saying something won't do any good. If she gets annoyed, it will only make things difficult for us and the kid. On the other hand, you could buy four or five tins of Bear Brand milk for her yourself. Where there's greed, it's not just over large sums of money. It can be just a few satang. When you think about it, it's sad. Here we are, a couple of prostitutes, and everyone looks down on us, including this couple, who've many times said disparaging things about us and who don't want to have anything to do with us. Yet it's strange, you know, they don't feel the slightest bit of shame at cheating us over the money for the baby's milk, which we earn from our sins, from doing something bad and disgusting in order to make a living. Huh! Sin it is that has to support virtue.'

Sixteen

THE problem of the small fiddle over the milk money was solved as Samorn suggested. Reun was not happy to see her child fall sick because of bad food, so some days, if she made a lot of money, she would stop off and buy milk she thought was suitable for the baby and take it round to Mae Peu-ut's. She told Mae Peu-ut she had just been passing and so had stopped off to buy it, so there was no need for Mae Peu-ut to buy it herself. But people who are by nature selfish are always on the look-out for personal gain, if not one way, then another, so they just cannot be trusted.

Rent day drew nearer. Samorn, who had not yet recovered, could scarcely bear to think about it. It was true that Reun went out to earn money in her place, but with the cost of milk and paying a baby minder, there was not enough left over for the rent. So as soon as Samorn felt that she was no longer feverish at night, she went out to help Reun earn money. With little sleep, however, and having only just recovered from one illness, Samorn's resistance was low and her health began to deteriorate once more. If she stopped work, there would not be enough money to pay the rent or support them. She forced herself to struggle on once more, but the very day after they had managed to scrape together enough money, Samorn collapsed exhausted on her bed. Gone was her strength, her spirit, and her hope of staying together with Reun.

No one could have been more grief-stricken than Reun. At first, after Samorn had fallen sick again, Reun rushed around looking after her as she had done previously. All day long she sat with her and comforted her. At night, when Samorn could manage to sleep by herself, Reun had to go out to work as before. If she did not, there would be no money for medicine. After several days, Samorn's condition took a turn for the worse and she could no longer be left alone at night. Reun had to stop going out and with a heavy heart she stayed at home with her. Samorn lay quietly on the bed, her sunken eyes gazing up at the roof of the mosquito net. Sometimes her fits of coughing and gasping would alternate in the most pitiful manner. Some days they would subside, almost as if she was getting better. At such times, she would lecture Reun, who remained constantly at her side, forgoing all sleep. Reun's gaze fixed on the sallow face before her and she responded solemnly but with full self-control.

There was hardly a tear in her eyes for her feelings for this woman whom she had come to think of as her own sister and who had been like a mother to her had left her emotionally exhausted. Samorn had loved her and helped her more than anyone else, but now she had no more to give.

During the night, Samorn woke with a start. She opened her eyes and saw Reun sitting there beside her. She attempted a weak smile and raised her head to drink the medicine from the glass Reun held out to her. Then she closed her eyes and was silent for a while. As the medicine began to take effect, her gasping and coughing eased. When she opened her eyes again, she felt strong enough to give a few parting instructions. She had to talk, but her voice was that of a sick person, interrupted frequently by bouts of coughing and exhaustion.

'I'm not going to make it beyond today or tomorrow. Dear Reun, without me, things are going to be difficult for you.'

Reun lifted her parched hand which was now little more than bone, and stroked it gently as she tried to comfort her. 'Don't go giving in, now, 'Morn. There's nothing very seriously wrong with you. Cheer up a bit and you'll soon be better and able to look after us again.'

Samorn shook her head slowly and answered in a low hoarse voice, scarcely more than a whisper. 'I know I'm not going to make it. There's nothing more for me to worry about apart from you. I'm really concerned that you'll have to start drifting around again on your own. Reun, promise me one thing, will you? Promise you'll do what I ask before I die?'

'Yes, I'll do what you say,' Reun agreed in a trembling voice.

'Give up this kind of work, do you hear, Reun. If there's a nice man to take care of you in the future, my soul will be happy and at peace, knowing that you have a husband and a home and don't have to drift about from place to place as you did when I was alive. Don't go following my example, with the label 'whore' stuck to you until the day you die. Don't do what I did, ending up with nothing, and having to sell my baby. My darling child ... he has no idea his mother is dying. His wretched mother ... who was so wicked she sold him to get the money to go and visit her husband.' She raved deliriously about her child, her arms grasping desperately at empty air and eyes rolling. Reun quickly grabbed her hands and held them tightly until Samorn returned to her senses, coughing two or three times and twisting with the pain in her chest.

'Reun, where are you?'

'I'm here. I won't leave you. I'm with you, right here.'

'Don't leave me. It won't be long before I die. My throat's so dry. Can you get me something to ease it?' Slowly and awkwardly, she propped herself up, and with a trembling hand, Reun poured a teaspoonful of the medicine she had used for Samorn's cough down the patient's throat.

'Oooh, that's really soothing, Reun. Is all our money gone yet? If it is,' Samorn added, becoming delirious once more, 'I'll go out and get some more.'

Reun just sat looking at her, choking back her feelings.

'Reun, pass me my skirt and blouse. What are you just sitting there for? Is there something the matter? I said I was going out to earn a bit of money. Khun Jit arranged to meet me at ... at ... I can't remember where.' She raised herself as if she was going to get up and Reun went to support her, tears of sadness streaming down her face.

''Morn, dear, just lie down now, OK?' Reun said, gently lowering her back down again. 'Where are you going off to?'

'I was just going to see who it was. There was someone knocking at the door, Reun. It's probably Khun Wit.' Reun's heart missed a beat and a shiver ran down her spine at the mention of Wit's name. 'Oh, no, it's not. I don't know who it is. Young Toi's so slow opening the door.' She paused and gasped and then continued deliriously. 'So you went and told Ba Taht that I kept all the money Khun Udom gave me myself, did you, Nang Win? Right then, I'm going to shove you down the stairs right now ... there!'

Samorn's condition remained the same throughout that day and night. Reun scarcely moved from her side, going without food and only drinking water like her sick companion. The day before, Mae Peu-ut had gone to call the doctor who had previously treated Samorn's fever, but he wouldn't come. He told her to find some other doctor, since the medicine he had prescribed was correct, and if it didn't do the trick, there was nothing else to be done except await the approach of death. And death really was approaching. Samorn's strength had all gone and even her speech had become indistinct. Her pulse was gradually getting weaker but she was still able to move a little despite the discomfort of breathing. All that remained was a sense of someone she really loved sitting beside her and watching over her. Samorn opened her eyes and looked at Reun. She stared at her with hardly a blink. Reun was startled when she began to choke for the first time, so violently, that her whole body shook and her eyes rolled upwards. Samorn opened her mouth to call for Mae Peu-ut, but no sound came as she choked again. She squeezed Reun's hand tightly and raised herself with a sigh.

''Morn! 'Morn!' Reun cried, distraught.

Samorn's hand gradually relaxed and her eyes which had been staring upwards lowered and closed tightly. As she opened her mouth and softly called Reun for the last time, she was seized by a third spasm of choking. The soul of Samorn, the prostitute who helped other people, departed from her body. It went quietly and peacefully. Reun bent closely over her. She did not cry loudly or wail so that others could hear. She collapsed numb beside the lifeless body. She was all alone now. Who else would give her the love and kindness that Samorn had? There was no one. This body would be gone. It would not be with her to care for her and comfort her and press money into her hands as it used to. Reun would have to fight hardship on her own.

On the advice of neighbours, Reun made arrangements for the body of her benefactress with little ceremony. She sold all of Samorn's things which she did not want herself. She did not need much now that there was just her. Suffering, loneliness, and missing Samorn almost drove Reun insane. Many times she wanted to take her own life, but when she thought of her innocent little child, she pulled herself together and kept going. She left the house in the morning and returned exhausted to her mosquito net late at night. She did not want to stay gazing at the emptiness around her, thinking, that was where 'Morn used to sleep, this was where she used to sit. She could not abandon her child and continued to see her as before. Whenever she picked her up, she always cried because it made her think of Samorn. There was no way she could keep her grief in check except by going out, wandering around the streets and lanes.

Some days, Reun would go and sit alone in the peace of Khao Din Park. She would gaze at the water in the lake and let her thoughts drift back to the home where she had once lived. She thought of her mother and father and brothers and sisters. Some nights, she would slip back to Ba Taht's house and stand outside, hidden by the dark, her eyes resting on the window of the room where she had once been happy with Wit, and where she had had Samorn to confide in. On other days, she would just wander around, stopping to buy something to eat when she was hungry, then drifting on again.

One day, Reun was wandering around aimlessly as usual. She turned into Werng Nakhon Khasem and was looking at what the Chinese shopkeepers had on sale. She was just looking with no intention of buying, happily picking up odd things and then putting them back again. As she was bending down looking at something in one shop, she heard a man with a strong provincial accent say to the Chinese shopkeeper, 'Hey, Towkay, how much is this, then?' It struck her that it was a voice she had heard before. She turned round quickly and her heart missed a beat, she was so pleased and excited. Surely, it was Feun, their neighbour. His face was no different from before. He was wearing green trousers, a short-sleeved shirt, and a *pakaoma* around his waist. He was holding up a carpenter's plane for the Chinese shopowner to see. He stared at Reun too, but did not recognize her. In her manner of dress and hairstyle, Reun no longer looked in the least bit like the Wahn of old, while her face retained only the slightest resemblance.

Reun stood there in amazement while he purchased the plane. She waited until Feun had put it under his arm before she stepped out after him. 'Feun, Feun!' she called.

He seemed startled that a woman's voice should be calling out his name. He turned round and looked suspicious when he saw Reun smiling at him. 'Was it me you were calling?' he asked, his expression showing no sign of recognition.

'Hey! Don't you remember me then, Feun? It's me, Wahn.' Feun thought for a moment. He looked her up and down from her hairstyle to the strange sarong she was wearing. From her appearance, it was clear that she was a prostitute, yet her face bore some resemblance to that of Wahn, the daughter of Ta Kert and Yai Im, who had run off with Khun Wichai that time. Yes, it really was Wahn. But why did she look like this?

'Oh, It's you, Wahn,' he greeted her with a shocked expression. 'Really, I almost didn't recognize you. Your hair looks all different. How's Bangkok then? OK?'

Reun's face clouded over immediately. 'Oh, not so bad,' she replied.

'Whereabouts are you living now?'

'In Worajak. When did you come to Bangkok?' Reun asked. She realized as she spoke that they were standing in the middle of the street so she suggested that they went and sat down in a teashop. She ordered two iced drinks and passed one to Feun.

Feun had still not recovered from the shock. Even though he was from the provinces, he understood Reun's present circumstances perfectly well. Looking at her, he felt sad. The Wahn who had once been beautiful with a full, charming face had gone pale and thin. He forgot what she had asked and she had to repeat her question.

'Oh yes. I've been here several days. How is Khun Wichai?' Feun mumbled. 'Is he all right?'

'Don't mention his name to me,' Reun said sharply. 'Let's just talk about Thepharat. How are my mother and father? Are they OK?'

Feun was on the point of telling her quite frankly, but then he felt sorry for her and did not have the heart to. 'Your mother's fine,' he mumbled half-heartedly.

Reun heaved a long sigh of relief when she learned that her parents were all right. 'If you go back, please tell them I'm fine, too. Tell them not to worry about me. That's all. I must be going now, Feun,' she said, laying the money for the drinks on the table and getting up. 'I've got one or two things to do elsewhere.'

Feun watched Reun with a look of pity. He half rose and called, 'Hang on a minute, Wahn. Don't go yet. I've got something to tell you.'

She turned round doubtfully, a look of sadness in her eyes. 'What is it, Feun?'

'You needn't leave any message for your parents,' he stammered, 'because they passed away a long time ago.'

'My mother and father dead?' Reun almost shouted.

'Yes,' said Feun.

Reun stood silent, rooted to the spot. She neither cried nor asked anything further. Slowly she turned round and walked out of the shop dazed. She carried on walking, without pausing, oblivious to the people who stopped and stared at her in astonishment. She did not care. Feun, the young fellow from her village, stood there stunned, watching until she disappeared from sight. Of course, once he got back to Thepharat district, he would go around telling everyone how the young and innocent Wahn had changed from a nice girl into a disgusting whore.

*   *   *

Reun raised her hands to shield her eyes from the car headlights which were shining in her eyes. The car sounded its horn to warn of the impending danger of being crushed beneath its wheels. She turned and bumped into something hard. She gripped it tightly to prevent her exhausted body from falling. She leaned over and looked down. Good Lord! It was so far down it made her feel giddy. She looked up and gazed around her. Where was she? She stared down to where her hands were tightly gripping something and then slowly her gaze extended further until....

Goodness! She was standing right in the middle of a bridge that crossed the river. She looked down over the side again. The swirling current beat against the concrete supports below, parting and flowing past on either side. Lights from both riverbanks reflecting on the surface of the water created a dazzling image, like the fire of suffering in her heart. As the current swept rapidly by, it created a circular pattern, like

Samorn's pale face lying on the pillow after her heart had stopped beating, the ripples forming her loose black hair. The face smiled invitingly, pleading with Reun to step down into peace and tranquility. She closed her eyes, feeling giddy, as if the vast, swirling waters had the power to drag her small, thin body down. She opened them once more and looked into the distance. The dark shadow of two cargo boats anchored in mid-river seemed like the huge form of a man and woman turning sullenly towards her. The two lanterns at the tops of the masts were like eyes blazing with anger, resentment, and a sense of loss. Reun buried her hands in her face. The souls of her mother and father were not yet sufficiently at rest to forget how heartless Reun had been when she had left. What else was there for Reun to enjoy? Her parents and even Samorn, who had supported her and been her closest friend, were dead. Having or not having a husband was all the same, for Wit had gone and she had little hope that he would return. Worst of all was the filth and evil in her body. As she thought about it, she felt she should not remain alive. It would be better to jump down into the water she saw swirling below than to continue a life of suffering and torture. She would let the powerful current wash away the filth and evil from her body and heart.

The car sounded its horn loudly once more. It was a sharp piercing sound which made Reun forget her desperate intention of taking her own life in cold blood. She stared after the large car as it drove slowly past her. From the light inside the vehicle she could clearly see a wealthy-looking lady whom she recognized from the day when Wit had rented a car and driven her out to eat in Ratchawong. This car had been parked alongside and Wit had pointed out a woman in the vehicle who was surrounded by men. 'It's Khunying Chertchoam,' he had whispered. 'Why should you be so ashamed of having to be a prostitute? Just look at the *khunying*, there. Is there anything about her that gives away her sordid past? In fact, Khunying Chertchoam used to be a prostitute like you, but she was fortunate and happened to become a *khunying*, complete with title, money, and servants. Do you think that all these things—wealth, high rank, and three daughters— can keep her on the straight and narrow? Not a chance. Now, as we watch her sitting up straight and looking at us with such contempt, she is a high-class whore with no morals and no sense of loyalty to her husband. Do you see, Reun? You're better than Khunying Chertchoam who deceives her husband behind his back and then puts on a show of affection to his face.'

A moment ago, Khunying Chertchoam had passed Reun in a car accompanied by several young men. Her face was bright and cheerful. But deep down she was tainted. There were even many more dozens of high-class ladies these days who, beneath honourable names, were much, much worse than Reun. Some had the title 'Chao' while others were 'Khunying', 'Khunnai', or 'Mom'. What of Reun? Of course, she had done something immoral, but was she the only one? There were many others. So why get upset to the point of thinking of killing oneself? Reun laughed wildly. She turned away from the bridge railing and made her way unsteadily back to the room she rented. She was ready to face up to whatever the future might hold.

Seventeen

LIFE alone in her old room, far from encouraginging a desire
to struggle on, had the exact opposite effect. Reun felt lonely
and disheartened. So after drifting around for a while, she
went to live with a friend who made her living in a similar
way. She left her child with Mae Peu-ut and Nai Klin as
before. Fate dictated that she entrust her child to the care of
others, for working made it impossible to look after her.

It was a new life she began, different from that she had led
in the past, where necessity had forced her into becoming a
prostitute. Even as a prostitute, she had cared about her reputation, and there had been Wit, the man she hoped would
take her away to a better future and for whom she had been
saving herself. But all that belonged to the past. Reun now
turned to prostitution, willingly and deliberately, no longer
saving herself for anyone. Yet there was still one life for
which she felt concern—that of her daughter. Otherwise, on
her own, she had nothing to fear from the world.

About ten days after she had moved from Worajak, she
went to see her daughter, taking with her the 6-baht payment for Mae Peu-ut. It was evening when she arrived at the
house. Had it been the Reun of old, the tears would have
been streaming down her face as she picked the baby up and
put her on her lap after an absence of ten days. Eet was visibly
thinner and she looked pale and unwell. Mucus trailed from
her nose, almost down to her mouth, and there were spots
and sores all over her skin. She had a hoarse cough.

'Aren't you well, Eet? What's the matter, dear?' Reun
asked as she bent over her little child. Eet was of course too
young to be able to talk or even understand what her own
mother was asking. She just looked up at her mother as if
pleading for help. Oh, God, thought Reun. My little darling,
I can see it in your eyes. Don't think I've just abandoned you.

I've been trying to find the money to look after you.

'Eet's not very well,' Mae Peu-ut said, bringing in the betel tray. 'She's got a cold. She's had a temperature for several days and it's only just beginning to go down today.' She sat down and put some betel in her mouth, apparently quite unconcerned about the child's condition.

'Have you taken her to a doctor?' Reun asked, upset by Mae Peu-ut's manner.

'What makes you think I haven't? I took her to the clinic but it didn't seem to do any good, so I took her to the doctor who's opened up over there,' she said, pointing over to the extreme right. 'I don't know what it was he said was the matter. Some foreign words he used. I can't remember. He was going to charge 5 or 6 baht to examine her and for medicine, so I didn't dare let him treat her.'

'Why on earth not? If you had, Eet might have been better by now,' said Reun.

'Because I didn't have any money,' Mae Peu-ut replied. 'Or,' she added in an offhand manner, 'would you have liked me to have sold Eet's necklace, then?'

Reun was no longer in full control of her temper and Mae Peu-ut's words infuriated her. 'You're not to do a thing with that necklace. If you hadn't got any money, why didn't you tell me? I'd have given you some. If she'd been really ill and you just kept quiet about it like this, would I have lost my child, then?' She put the child down from her lap and sadly kissed its grubby cheek again. There was no point in making a scene. She handed Mae Peu-ut some money. 'I'll bring the money for the doctor's fees and the medicine tomorrow,' she added.

Long after she returned to where she was staying, Reun still had no idea where she was going to get the money from. Seeing her so restless, her friends asked what the matter was and learned that she needed 5 or 6 baht.

'Hey, don't be silly. You know that Indian fellow who comes here quite often? He came that day we were sitting out round the front of the house. The one who chased the dogs away after he'd parked his bike.'

'Oh yes, I remember,' said Reun. 'What am I supposed to do with him then?'

'He lends money. He's downstairs talking to Mae Choey at the moment. Try and work something out with him. Be careful, though, Reun, his interest is really high.'

Reun was on her feet immediately. 'I don't care how much it costs. All I want is the money. It's for my kid, you know, Sam-ang. She's sick.'

The loan was subsequently agreed at an interest rate of 20 per cent, which, moreover, had to be paid on a daily basis. If it had not been for the fact that her child was sick and in need of her help, Reun would never have allowed herself to submit to such extortion at the hands of a foreigner. It was not so much a case of how much money, as just being able to get hold of it that really mattered. It was because of this money that Eet was now getting better by the day. Her mother's health, in contrast, was suffering as a result of the exorbitant 20 per cent interest, and she would probably be just skin and bones by the time she finished paying off the debt.

'Reun, you're getting so thin. Why don't you give yourself a rest,' Mae Choey, her employer, suggested. 'Just look at you. You're so skinny!' Mae Choey showed rather more care and concern for her girls than Ba Taht.

'Yes, maybe I'll take two or three days off,' Reun replied. 'But I don't want to be a nuisance.' Reun always showed the utmost respect and consideration for those who treated her well.

Mae Choey did her job better than Ba Taht. She was like

one of the girls and not at all strict. The younger girls liked and respected her, and whatever they earned, they gave her. Moreover, she looked after them and gave them advice on all kinds of things. She didn't let them go around in old shabby things, but rather, had them wear nice, brightly coloured clothes. It was this kind of thing which won her the hearts of those in her charge. When she heard Reun's words, she beat her hand against her breast. 'My goodness, what d'you mean, Reun, you don't want to be a nuisance? Have a break. There are plenty of others who are fit and strong. Take a break right away. That'll be good, too, because now we're nearing the end of the month, there aren't many people coming.' As she finished speaking, Mae Choey glanced over towards the door where a middle-aged woman had appeared, unnoticed, and seemed to be looking for someone. 'Who's she looking for?' she asked.

Reun looked over in the same direction. 'It's me she's come to see,' she said, rising to meet Mae Peu-ut. Mae Peu-ut, it seemed, had come to ask for more money to buy tinned milk for Eet, because the money Reun had given her last time would run out that evening. Reun looked at her suspiciously. It was exactly ten days ago that she had given her the money for six tins of milk There was no way it could all be gone. On average, one tin lasted just under two days.

'Hey! Why's it gone so quickly?' Reun demanded, unable to restrain herself. 'Eet seems to have been drinking less milk as she's got older.' Such *naïveté* would prompt a mocking laugh from a cheat.

'No, that's not why it's all gone. Eet, the little rascal, keeps tipping the can over,' Mae Peu-ut explained. 'If you can't get me the money, shall I let her go without milk, then? She is nearly nine months now.' Mae Peu-ut knew that Reun loved her child and would not want her to go without milk. She was simply trying to provoke Reun.

'I'm not having her go without milk because I can still afford it. Go home now and come back and pick it up tomorrow. Make sure you come early, too.' Reun's curt reply was sufficient to raise Mae Peu-ut's hopes of getting the money. In fact, there was still some milk left, but she needed the money for betting on the horses at the Nang Lerng race track, the following afternoon, Saturday. There was nowhere she could get any money, so she planned to use the milk money from Reun.

Reun went back inside, looking downcast. That was the end of any thoughts of having a rest today. She confided her troubles to Mae Choey. There was only one hope and that was that she would have to find a customer tonight in order to get the money for at least two tins of milk. Mae Choey offered sympathy. 'Right,' she said, 'today I'll find you a customer with a nice fat wallet.'

True to her word, Mae Choey did find a customer with a nice fat wallet. It was an Indian, the owner of a draper's shop in Pahurat. Reun almost died with shock. Inwardly she wept. He was enormous, just like some great ape from India, with a loud voice and bushy whiskers. Even worse, he did not bother to bath or wash himself like other people. She went to meet her Indian benefactor with the loud mouth and then re-treated in revulsion. Then she thought of her dear child. Eet was her last remaining treasure. There was no one else in the world except her dear, dear Eet. She pulled herself together and went in again. She laughed loudly to cover up her sadness.

*   *   *

Among the teeming crowds struggling to buy tickets at the race track next day could be seen Mae Peu-ut, the wife of Nai Klin. Red-faced, she was pushing her way through people in front, holding up five 1-baht notes and shouting to the man selling tickets. The sight of banknotes being held up in the midst of such a crowd might have saddened the observant onlooker if he or she had known that they were the banknotes Reun had got by forcing herself to sell sex when she was unwell in the belief that her daughter was starving. Sin it was that supported virtue.

After resting until she was a little better, Reun had to return to work once more. She put the pain and suffering out of her mind when she realized that she would have to continue to face this life. Sometimes she thought about Samorn's words of advice, just before she died, about finding a good husband and settling down. Reun had intended to keep her promise to Samorn for the child's sake, but as far as she herself was concerned, her feelings for Wit remained as strong as ever. She loved him and she did not want anyone else to take his place. Although she tried to convince herself that he was dead, she still waited. She took a careful look at every man who came her way. Some said they loved her and begged her to go and live with them, but she had no wish to do so, for by now, she was a good judge of men. Her first mistake had been an effective enough lesson. They were the kind of men who lived off women. They would go around the brothels smartly dressed, their pockets full of money, making friends with the best-looking girls. Then they would set the girl up at home and force her to earn money which they then used to indulge themselves further and to ruin more women.

Some of the men were young and unsuccessful in love. Others were already married and were escaping from their wives for a bit of fun. Reun knew nearly everything about all these men. Several were royal princes. With her very own eyes, Reun had seen them going into theatres with sweet young princesses and everyone bowing respectfully to them. Then, a few nights later, the same prince would be mingling with the likes of her into the small hours, having bribed the driver to tell the beautiful princess that 'His Highness has gone to his club.'

Some people came who you would never have thought would visit prostitutes. One such case was a judge. He was reputed to be the finest, and in his hands lay the powers to mete out justice. He was honoured by all. At work he occupied a large office with an electric ceiling fan. He had people at his command. At home, his wife and children went in awe of him. But once inside a brothel, his manner changed. Girls tugged at his moustache, flung their arms around his neck from all sides, stroked his head, and rubbed his back at will. Why did all this go on? Who can say? Even the judge himself, in quiet moments, would murmur, 'What on earth's got into me? I'm neither man nor monkey.'

Then there were the doctors, who preached to the people about the dangers of venereal diseases. They would stand in the midst of audiences of hundreds, speaking in a serious tone of voice. When they reached the point of urging all men to abandon their visits to prostitutes, their voices would tremble and they would put on a sorrowful expression as they spoke of the horrors of the disease and how it might spread even to their own sons and grandsons. Yet who would have guessed that these doctors themselves frequented the premises of prostitutes nearly every day.

There were other things which made you think even more, which actually concerned Reun herself. That day Mae Choey called her down and introduced her to a young man of only twenty-three or twenty-four. He had a clear complexion with distinct features and had just returned from Singapore. After chatting with him for a while, Mae Choey asked him why he had returned to Bangkok instead of finishing his studies.

He laughed. 'My father was afraid I'd be ruined by too many nights on the town,' he replied, 'so he called me back. But this kind of thing goes on wherever you are.'

'Doesn't he know that you've come here to see us, then?' Reun asked.

The young man shook his head. 'He has no idea. He said that if I disobeyed him and went to brothels, he'd smash my head in with his own hands.'

'Good gracious,' said Mae Choey, 'is he that vicious?'

'Like a tiger. Even with his own children. If the servants upset him, he boots them.'

The young man was himself frightened when he spoke of his father.

Before he could say another word, there were sounds of heavy footsteps entering the house. Mae Choey got up to see who it was. 'Oh, it's Khun Phra. Do please come in, sir.'

As Khun Phra entered the living-room, the young man who had arrived earlier and who was now laughing and joking with Reun turned round and looked at him. Immediately something occurred which no one would have dreamed possible. Momentarily taken aback, Khun Phra picked up a stick and advanced on the young man. 'You little devil,' he bellowed, 'Didn't I tell you never to go near a brothel?'

The son jumped up, grabbed the hand in which his father held the stick, and hung on tightly. 'What's so unusual?' he shouted back. 'If you can come, Father, so can I.'

Reun sat watching father and son thinking what a pitiful sight it was. Here was a father teaching his son not to go to prostitutes even though he himself was virtually a regular here. What was more, a father, renowned for being as fierce as a tiger, came here like a nice tame cat. Who was right, who wrong? If adults teach their children not to do something that is wrong and then do it themselves, what happens to authority within the home? She closed her eyes and thought of the restrictions that customs imposed upon daughters. But they were merely for the sake of appearances. Who could ever be a partner for Reun? She had no wish to damage the lives of those she admired. So she continued her life as before, even though she had not forgotten Samorn's dying words.

Eighteen

THE sound of *pinphat* music coming from Wat Thepharat echoed out along the river, urging the villagers of Thepharat to hurry from their homes to hear the monks chanting and to call their children and paddle or row their boats to the distant temple with trays of food offerings. When the bell had stopped ringing, the monks emerged from their cells and made their way to the prayer pavilion for the annual Songkran festival. The sunlight shining through the hanging branches of the banyan tree on to the bright saffron robes of the monks caught the eyes of the devout who sat listening in rows in the pavilion according to traditional custom.

A young village girl in a reddish striped skirt and cream silk blouse sat by the eastern balustrade of the temple pavilion preparing an offering of flowers, incense, and candles. Hearing some of the old folk murmuring that the monks were coming, she looked up. Then she turned and nudged her friend who was sitting beside her.

'Jan, Jan,' she said, 'Look at that woman sitting by the jetty.'

The girl who had been nudged craned her neck to have a look. 'Where? I can't see anyone.'

'What's the matter? Are you blind or something? Over there, sitting by herself, wearing a dark purple sarong and with nice curly hair. She must be from Bangkok. It's funny, she looks worn out.'

Just as Jan caught sight of the woman, they heard a man's deep bass voice reciting the precepts. An old hunchbacked woman sitting next to them with her head bowed and hands clasped together turned and whispered to them to be quiet before resuming her former position as she listened to the recitation. Jan was going to get Nuan to point her out again, but when the chance arose, the woman whom the Thepharat village girls had seen had disappeared. She had got up while the village folk were listening to the precepts and gone to stand where she had a good view of everyone and everything that was going on at the Songkran festival without any of the villagers being able to get a close look at her. She watched the girls hurrying to fill the monks' alms bowls with rice from their polished stone bowls. They looked different from two years earlier and they were dressed more like city people. Yet this scene of young girls and young and old folk all squeezed and crushed against each other as they served rice to the monks was no different from before. The man making all that noise was Ta Dee. She still recognized him. The middle-aged woman leading her child out of the pavilion was Pii Norm, and that girl with the rice bowl in front of her friends—surely it was Noo Soy, Lung Saeng's daughter. Last time she had seen her, she wasn't this beautiful. Thepharat was very different from before—so much so that not a single person recognized that the woman standing there, a little apart, watching with sad eyes, was Wahn, the daughter of Ta Kert and Yai Im, who on that Songkran festival had joined in the merit-making, serving rice to the monks just like them.

Suddenly, her heart missed a beat. Seeing Feun wandering over towards the dilapidated pavilion with two or three friends, she quickly sat down out of sight. Wahn had once seen Feun sitting with the man she never, at the time, dreamed would deceive her so utterly. She looked at everyone there. Only her parents, her very own mother and father, and her two brothers were missing. She could no longer hold back her tears when she thought of her mother and father who must have died broken-hearted because of her, their daughter. What about Pii Wang and Noo Wing? Why hadn't they come to offer food at the temple? Or was it that.... She closed her eyes. She did not want to think about it. The past was too painful, so painful that she almost wished she were dead.

Slowly and absent-mindedly, she walked away from the temple, across the high wooden bridge to the other side of the river, and then turned left along the dike. Although the sun burned down fiercely, the heat causing her to squint, Reun remained unperturbed. She was heading straight for her home—the home where mother and father, daughter and sons had once lived happily together. From the *sakae* thicket, it used to be possible to see the palm-thatched roof quite clearly. But here she was, some way beyond the bushes, and there was no sign of it. Just emptiness. She stepped on to the threshing yard where once she used to pile up the sheaves of rice. She cast a glance around the compound with a feeling of sorrow. Her parents' house was gone. It had all been taken down. The compound had been left deserted, tangled and overgrown with vines while the upper branches of the *sa-noh* bush swayed too and fro. It was quiet except for the sound of the breeze blowing against two or three clumps of bamboo growing along the top of the dike. She slumped to the ground as if she were exhausted. Her eyes filled with tears as she gazed ahead, her heart pounding in dismay. She had come back to see the place where she had once lived happily with her parents. It was now deserted and overgrown with tall grass that swayed in the breeze. Inside she felt desolated. Once it had been neat and tidy because there was somebody to tend it. Early in the morning her father used to lead their two water-buffaloes out past where Reun now stood, to graze on the grass and rice straw on the threshing ground by the *sa-noh* bushes. In the cold season, they would all sit down together as a family warming themselves around a fire. In her mind, she could still see the two small houses quite clearly.

*   *   *

Even the wooden bed which had been put underneath the tamarind tree to relax on was no longer there. Father used to sit propped up there in a *pakaoma*, gazing out over the canal, watching the boats paddling up and down. When he saw someone he knew, he would shade his eyes and shout a greeting the way old folk do. She looked up at the tamarind tree at the water's edge, her face bathed in tears. It was all that was left to see of her old home in this, her time of loss. Wahn used to get her younger brother, Wing, to climb the tree and pick the tender leaves at the top and put them into a bag, fashioned out of cloth, around his neck. He used to climb every branch, inching his way to the very top of the tree, and he would swing from branch to branch, as agile as anything, while he sang, 'Sao oey ja bork hai'. When he had filled the bag with young leaves, he would bring them down and wash them. Then the leaves were boiled with the head of dried *chorn* fish to make a sharp-tasting and rather salty soup, or else put into onion shrimp paste and pounded very finely. When Father sipped a spoonful of this warm soup, he would murmur, 'Mmm, that goes down a treat.'

When the pods appeared, Wahn used to collect them and wrap them in banana leaves and place them by the jetty. Passers-by would buy them for pounding into chilli paste to eat with rice. When the green pods turned a dark brown colour, Mother would take a look at them and then organize her three children to pick them and then put them out in the sun to dry. When evening came, there was nothing to do, so Mother would sit shelling the tamarind seeds with a small knife and arranging them in rows in the winnowing basket while she listened to Pii Wang reading from *Phra Aphaimani* which she had rented in several volumes. Father would lie with his legs stretched out on a pillow, his lips moving as if he were talking to himself, while his eyes remained fixed on the palm-thatched roof. He was neither praying nor grumbling about anyone, but rather counting how many cartloads of rice he had sold and how much he had left in the barn. Wing would sit with both legs stretched out, moulding the soft clay into round pellets of equal size which he would sell to Ta Suk for shooting at crows.

Now, however, the tamarind tree which had once served its owner so well stood there sadly. Its leaves were dry and had turned red. Many of the branches were bare and the tree itself was leaning over into the canal. It looked as if it had already fallen down and was counting the days before someone came and cut off its branches for firewood. Reun turned back to the left where there was a mass of overgrown grass. That was where her mother had once dug up the ground to grow luffa and pumpkins and after that it had been the buffalo enclosure. But now it was gone. Everything was gone ... except silence and emptiness.

Reun wiped her tear-stained face, rose to her feet, and walked back through the overgrown grass. She crossed the same wooden bridge and made straight for the house which used to belong to Lung Sorn and Ba Porng—that same house where she had gone to play cards that Songkran day. Now, perhaps, it belonged to someone else. Reun wanted to see whoever lived there so that she could ask for news of her brothers. A dog lay at the front of the house, breathing noisily. Hearing the sound of approaching footsteps in the dry undergrowth, it pricked up its ears. In a moment it saw the stranger and with a fierce growl, it rose to its feet and ran forward, barking menacingly.

'Ai Daen! What are you barking for?' A woman in an old black sarong pulled up high to her knees and an old, dirty, patterned *pa taep* waddled out from the back of the house, her hands holding her swollen stomach. Her gaze fell upon the stranger standing there in the heat of the sun, with Ai Daen looking as if he was about to go and bite her. She looked at the stranger suspiciously. Then, without further ado, she quickly picked up a stick and ran out chasing the dog away. 'Be off with you! Ai Daen! Go on, away! There. He's gone now. Who do you want to see?' she asked when she got nearer, near enough for the two of them to be able to see each other's face clearly. 'Come into the shade a bit. You're right in the sun there.'

Whoever was it? Reun looked closely at the woman's face. It really was Poom, Lung Sorn and Ba Porng's daughter. She used to be such an attractive girl. Now she looked completely different, with her clothes all dirty and her protruding stomach. Having once been close to Poom, to come back after so long and find her in this state, and then for her not to even recognize Reun, filled Reun with sadness. She stood there stunned for a moment until Poom called her again.

Poom looked closely at the stranger and the clothes she was wearing. 'You're from Bangkok, I suppose?' she said.

'Yes,' replied Reun, quietly. She had not taken her eyes off the other woman. She was on the point of saying, 'Poom! It's me, Wahn! Don't you recognize me? It's Wahn, who used to be your friend. Who used to work in the rice fields with you. We used to go and watch them playing *kao pii ling* in Yai Chaeng's paddy fields, remember?' She sighed deeply as she thought of the game of *kao pii ling* that Songkran day.

'Has any particular reason brought you here?' asked the woman who had once been Reun's playmate. 'Please go up into the house and sit yourself down. If we stand around here, Ai Daen will soon be back snapping at your feet.' She could not help wondering why this Bangkok woman behaved almost as if she knew her. There was no one in her family who lived in Bangkok. She suppressed her curiosity and led the way up to the house. She took out a brass betel bowl and placed it in front of them. Then she removed the lid from a glass jar which stood partly concealed by the house post and took out a betel leaf which she folded in two.

Reun waited until the owner of the house had settled before introducing herself in the way she had planned. 'I'm a distant relative of Lung Kert and Ba Im. I've come from Bangkok to pay a brief visit. Isn't that where their house was?' she asked, pointing to where her old home had once stood. She struggled to hold back her tears when she mentioned her parents' names. 'I don't know what's happened to it.'

'Oh, you're a relative of Lung Kert and Na Im, are you? No wonder. The moment I saw you I thought you looked like Na Im. Right there. That's where their house was. It was taken down this last harvest.'

'Why was it taken down?' Reun asked in a trembling voice. 'Did they go and live somewhere else?'

'Oh, you probably didn't hear that Lung Kert and Na Im died, did you?' the woman asked, looking straight at Reun.

Reun shook her head slowly. Tears streamed down her cheek. Poom's eyes reddened too. She had no doubt that this Bangkok woman really must be a relative of the couple. Otherwise, why would she be so grief-stricken when she heard the news of their death? Poom was herself a close neighbour. She knew everything that had gone on in that family. Realizing that this woman wanted news of her relatives, she set about telling Reun without further prompting.

'It was a real shame about them. If things had been different, they would surely have lived longer. They would never have gone so quickly. It was because they were so upset about their daughter, Wahn. You must know her. She ran off with some man, you know. Wahn and I were very close. She was such a good kid. She shouldn't have done it, running away with him like that. Do you ever come across her in Bangkok? Someone who bumped into her not long ago told me she was a prostitute now. Dear me!'

These words sent a shiver to Reun's heart. Scarcely able to face such a truth, she was about to defend herself. But on reflection, she realized that everything Poom said was true. She was a prostitute, just as people said. So she controlled herself and continued to listen.

'Two or three days after her daughter ran off with that man, Na Im fell ill. She was upset. Wahn hadn't just gone off with him. She'd taken all the family valuables with her. Na Im was ill for two or three months and then she died. I wasn't at home. I'd gone out to plant rice and I didn't get back until evening. My father told me she'd died. She'd gone to have a look at the tamarind tree. She was looking around there, or something, when she collapsed and died. It was too late to do anything. He said that the day she died, she'd been grumbling about her daughter all day long. Once Wahn had gone, things were very difficult for her. She had to cook her own food even though she wasn't very strong. Her other two kids were a dead loss. Good-for-nothing lads.' As she spoke, she looked at the woman sitting before her. She saw her sob frequently, and began to cry herself, not suspecting in the least that this woman was Wahn, the daughter of Lung Kert and Na Im, for she bore no resemblance whatsoever to Wahn. Poom paused to compose herself before continuing.

'They had not even cremated Na Im when Lung Kert died as well. He died of drink. He was depressed, thinking about his wife and daughter. There was nothing he could do, so he turned to drink. And he drank himself to death. That left just Wang and Wing. They couldn't get the money together for their parents' cremation, so they agreed to sell their land to the Chinese towkay, Hak Long. They got the money and had the cremation for their parents and then they moved out. Where they went, north or south, I couldn't say. No one's heard anything of them. The towkay came and pulled the house down last harvest. All because of Wahn. If it hadn't been for her, none of this would have happened.'

The more Reun heard, the worse it made her feel. It was indeed because of her, as Poom said, that her parents had died, one after the other, and her brothers had gone off on their own separate ways. No sooner had she dried her eyes than tears began to trickle down her face again. Their home was gone and all their land now belonged to someone else. She stared at what had once been theirs and shuddered.

'It was their karma that the mother and father should die and Wahn should become a prostitute. She didn't like living with decent parents. She had to be different. By the way,' Poom added, 'where are you staying?'

Reun dared not look up to answer the question. She mumbled something, so that all Poom caught was 'I'm staying at Klong Suan market and I'm going back to Bangkok tomorrow. I was coming to visit them, but they're not here.'

Originally, she had intended to walk as far as Yai Chaeng's threshing ground where all her troubles and those of her family had begun, but she had to abandon the idea. The sad news she had heard from Poom a moment earlier had affected her very much. Her mother had died in the same position as when she used to poke her head up and tell her children to gather the ripe tamarind pods. Before leaving her old home, she walked up to the trunk of the tamarind tree and buried her face against one of its branches. A small bird suddenly flew from the bushes with a cry, like the chilling voices of her parents chiding her. Oh, Mother. I was wrong. Go on, curse me. I accept it was all my fault.

*   *   *

Worn out, Reun went back to where she was staying. The next day she took the mail boat back to Bangkok. Her intention in returning to Thepharat had been to ease the misery and sense of loneliness that tortured her, in the same way that anyone who has put up with a lot of suffering wants to see and think about things and places which once gave them happiness. But it had not worked out that way. Instead of having her battered spirits raised, Reun had returned to hear herself cursed for bringing ruin and destruction to her home and family. Even as she sat there on the boat, none of her fellow travellers could resist casting a scornful glance in her direction. Some even whispered to each other, just loud enough for her to hear, 'There you are! A prostitute coming up-country to work.' They were strong words, like fuel smouldering eternally in her breast.

Nineteen

REUN'S life did not just end there at that point. It had to go on. But once she had taken this course, there could be no hope of future happiness. All there was to look forward to, whether to a greater or lesser extent, was sorrow and misery.

Mae Choey's place was where Reun worked longer than anywhere else. However, as she got older, she began to lose her looks. She grew thin and no longer looked fresh and attractive like the younger girls. Her earnings, which had already fallen, became more meagre still. She was unable to earn enough to make ends meet. A certain amount she set aside for her child's care. What was left did not go very far. Reun could not put up with the poverty in silence. It was an endless struggle to make enough. Bangkok had become stifling. It was difficult to make a living there. When friends invited her to go up-country, Reun agreed, not simply because of the money, but also because she wanted to see how the lives of rural people differed from those of people in the city. People often said that rural folk were not very ambitious, that their way of life was unexciting and very quiet and peaceful. Peace was exactly what she wanted; where there was peace, that was where she wanted to be.

Reun travelled around plying her trade in various provinces. First she went south, to Ratchburi, Petchburi, and as far as Prachuab Khirikhan. But she did not seem to earn any more money than before. Then, with friends, she went back north, as far as Nakhon Sawan, where she stayed about a year, which was longer than she stayed anywhere else. In the end she found she was less happy than she had been in Bangkok. Up-country, whenever she saw a child about the same age as Eet, it immediately made her think of her own dear child. Throughout the four years that she was moving around from one place to the next, her child must have been growing up quickly. What is more, people had said that it was better up-country than in the city because people were not ambitious. Reun had seen with her very own eyes that it was not true. Up-country people had to live a quiet and peaceful existence because progress had not yet reached that far. The farmers who complained of their own poverty and suffering condemned city folk as wasteful and extravagant for the way they accumulated material possessions. In fact, in this respect, rice farmers were just the same. When she had lived in Thepharat, Reun had known little about life; but having reached an age when she was capable of thinking for herself, she had begun to understand. It was true that farmers such as her mother and father and relatives had to toil away in the rice fields, bathed in their own sweat before they got the grains of rice. But did they get as much benefit out of the rice they produced for the efforts that they had put in? Once the rice had been harvested, they would simply stay at home resting, claiming that they had worked hard enough. They would measure out the unhusked rice in their barn and sell it so that they could buy gold jewellery. If city people had gold belts, then farmers would sell their rice and buy the same. Some even went out of their way to sell rice so that they could gamble away the money at cards. So what was all this about not being ambitious? It wasn't like that any more.

Reun was happiest in Bangkok, where her darling little child was waiting. So she left Nakhon Sawan—the last place on her wanderings—and returned in search of the happiness she craved. She went back to live with Mae Choey on Ratchadamnoen Klang Road, the latter being quite happy to welcome her home again. She arrived back during the day, but had scarcely time to rest before thoughts of her daughter prompted her to quickly get dressed and leave the house again.

Mae Peu-ut and Nai Klin had moved from Worajak about a year earlier. Reun remembered receiving a letter from Nai Klin when she first went to live in Nakhon Sawan telling her that they had moved from Worachak to Bang Krabeu and asking her to send school fees and the keep for her daughter via Post Office Number 7. Finding Mae Peu-ut and Nai Klin's house was not very difficult after she had asked two or three people in the vicinity. 'That one over there,' they said, directing her towards the green house standing in a row of single-storey homes. 'The one where they sell bananas and pomelos.'

Reun walked over in the direction indicated until she reached the house where they sold fruit. Mae Peu-ut was sitting there alone with her back turned, engrossed in her work. Hearing the sound of loud footsteps approaching, she guessed it was probably someone coming to buy something.

She turned round quickly and saw Reun standing there, smiling, right next to her.

'Good grief! I thought I heard someone. And it's you, Reun! When did you get down from Nakhon Sawan?' she greeted her warmly because she had not seen her for nearly four years. 'Do sit down.'

Once seated, Reun stared inside the house. 'I only got in today. Where's Eet?'

'She's at school. They'll be out soon. She's full of herself now. So much to say for herself, and so bright. She's not afraid of standing up to anyone, either. But what about Nakhon Sawan then? Was it all right there?'

Reun told her what it had been like in that province as well as she could, turning towards the front of the house several times as she spoke. She badly wanted to see her child. Moments later came the sound of a child's footsteps running noisily from the left-hand side of the house. The clear voice of a child reached her ears. Mae Peu-ut nodded to indicate that it was the voice of Reun's child. Reun's heart pounded fiercely. It was more than four years since she had last seen her child.

A skinny little child wearing a one-piece trouser suit rushed into the room. In one hand she was carrying her lessons and in the other a bundle that looked like a single tiffin bowl. As soon as she saw the strange woman standing there smiling at her, the little girl suddenly came to a startled halt; and when she saw the strange woman approaching with outstretched arms, as if she was going to hug her, she began to back away.

'Mummy,' she cried, looking towards Mae Peu-ut.

Tears came to Reun's eyes at her first clear sight of her child, at the sight of her pale, thin body and smooth face. Jet-black eyes looked up suspiciously at Reun. She had been away only four years and now when she came back, she found her child grown into this slender little creature. But her daughter did not recognize her. Indeed, she called the woman who looked after her, Mae Peu-ut, 'Mummy' and even looked as if she was afraid of her real mother. Slowly, Reun lowered the arms she had held out towards her child. She felt sad and rejected. Seeing this, Mae Peu-ut immediately reprimanded the child. 'Eet, why won't you go to your mother then? Don't you remember Reun? She doesn't remember you because she was only just starting to walk when you went up-country. Look, that's your mummy, dear.'

A small pair of eyes stared into the face of this strange woman. Mae Peu-ut had to reprimand her again before she approached the woman, hesitantly and suspiciously. She had always called Mae Peu-ut 'Mummy'. So why was there another 'mummy'? The more she saw the tears streaming down Reun's face, the more doubtful she felt. She stared first at Mae Peu-ut, then at Reun.

Reun grabbed the child and clasped her tightly to her, as if she feared she might run away. She kissed her lovingly all over her face—on her cheeks, her eyebrows, and her chin. Her darling child! She looked so like her father. Reun felt her hair. It was so fine and soft. And her hands and her skin, they were so soft, too. Reun felt something hard as she stroked her chest. Slowly she pulled it out and as she looked closely at it her thoughts turned to Wit. How would he feel if he knew his own flesh and blood was as lovely as this? She hugged and kissed her little child excitedly for a moment. Then, in a trembling voice, she whispered, 'Do you know I'm your mummy?'

Eet shook her head. 'No, I only have that mummy,' she replied softly, nodding in the direction of Mae Peu-ut. Mae Peu-ut sat watching in surprise and with some unease. Even though she had exploited Reun before, the child was so sweet that she loved her as if she were her own. Now, seeing mother and daughter embracing, she could not help but feel sorry for them, no matter how hard-hearted she was.

'I'm your mummy who looks after you and that's your real mummy, right? That's your proper mummy, OK? She asked me to look after you,' Mae Peu-ut explained, pointing first to herself and then to Reun, so that Eet would understand.

The child looked at the woman holding her once more, as if to ask, 'Is it true what Mae Peu-ut says?' And then overcome by the power of the bond of blood between them, her lips broke into a happy smile and she pressed her tiny cheek against her mother's arms. What really struck Reun about Eet was her calm and gentle manner. She had the blood of the gentry, the blood of her father. Eet remained silent for a while and then she looked up. 'Where have you been, Mummy?' she asked hesitantly, feeling shy and self-conscious at calling Reun 'Mummy'. Such an innocent question was like a knife in Reun's heart. It was some time before she could answer. 'I've been earning money so that you could go to school. How far have you got in your reading?'

'I'm up to *sara* "a",' she said with childish affectation. 'Teacher says I'm a good reader.'

Reun bent down and gave her a kiss. 'Will you read me something?' she asked. 'I'd like to hear you.' If Reun had not been a prostitute, little Eet would have been the pride and joy of parents and grandparents, with her sweet little mouth and nose. She would have been surrounded by members of the family who would have loved her and shielded her from even the slightest trouble.

'I don't want to read now. I read at night-time. Why don't you come and sleep with me at night?'

A lump rose in Reun's throat and she swallowed hard before replying. 'I'm busy so I can't come and sleep with you. You must work very hard at school and then I'll come and sleep with you.' Then, looking up towards Mae Peu-ut, she said, 'Please make sure that Eet does her lessons. Please, for my sake. I don't care how poor I am. All I ask is that Eet gets an education like other people's children.'

'Don't worry, Reun. I bring her up just as if she were really mine. Even though you didn't write from Ratchburi telling me to take Eet to school, I'd already made up my mind once she could speak properly that I was going to send her to school.'

'Oh, Mae Peu-ut, I'm so grateful to you for that,' Reun said. She gazed down at her child's legs. 'What's this? Let's have a look at your feet. Don't you wear shoes when you go to school?' Her little legs were covered in sores, some of which were full of pus, while others had burst and were oozing a yellow liquid.

'Eet's shoes are ripped,' Mae Peu-ut hastened to reply, 'so she hasn't got any to wear to school. She's got ant bites all over her. Her skin is so soft.'

'Right. Tomorrow I'm going to buy you some shoes. What colour would you like?' Reun asked, feeling pity for her daughter.

'I want red ones, like Paeo's. Paeo's got red shoes,' Eet replied quickly. Her great black eyes shone with happiness. 'And Paeo's got a bag for her books, too.' Her tiny hands grasped her mother by her upper arms, and she looked up, eager to know whether her mother would get her what she wanted.

'Tomorrow, I'll get them for you,' Reun told her daughter. 'Red shoes and a small bag for your books. But you must work hard at school, right?'

Eet was thrilled when she heard her mother promise to buy the things. Almost as if she had been taught to do so, she snuggled up against her mother, wrapped her arms around her and hugged her tightly. 'I love you so much, Mummy.'

When she heard her daughter's words, Reun's tears fell upon the sleek hair spread against her breast. Who had told or taught the child to try to please her mother this way? You mustn't love me, my darling, I'm not good enough for you to love. I'm bad. Do you realize that? Mae Peu-ut could stand it no longer. She wiped away her tears with the edge of her *pa taep* and then rose and went inside.

Reun remained with her daughter until evening. She felt sad as she returned from Mae Peu-ut's. She had kissed her daughter so lovingly and then kissed her again. She turned back to see her child standing there waving and her heart sank. The words, 'I love you so much, Mummy,' still rang fresh in her ears. Oh, Wit. How delighted you would be if you could see how lovely your little child is. Would you mind that Eet's mother is a prostitute? I envy Mae Peu-ut so much at being able to bring her up, to hear her first words, and to be loved as a mother by Eet. And here I am, Eet's real mother, loving her so desperately, suffering every hardship to earn enough money to support her and then having no chance to be with her. I have to be so far from her.

Reun looked away as a woman approached with her daughter. Reun had a daughter just like that woman. But she never took her out anywhere like other people. Who was to blame that she was a prostitute?

Reun did not forget what it was her daughter wanted. She thought that in the evening she would be able to earn enough to be able to go and buy them. But her hopes went unfulfilled, for as it happened, there were no clients at all. The next day, out of love for her daughter and a wish to please her, Reun gathered together a number of her silk skirts. She left the house and went straight to the pawnshop where she exchanged them for more than 4 baht. Then she went to Pahurat and bought a pair of red shoes in her daughter's size. She also bought some material with a lovely delicate floral pattern to have it sewn into a blouse for Eet to wear to school. Then she went on to Ban Mor and called in at a shop where they made leather bags. While she was making her selection, she heard a commotion out on the street and she turned her gaze from the bags to the direction the noise was coming from. A crowd of nearly a hundred was hurrying up to see two police officers handcuffing a man and marching him away, close to where she was standing. The prisoner's body was blood-stained all over and the crowd sounded full of hatred. Even from a distance, Reun could scarcely stand the sight of blood. But when the policemen led their victim right past her so that she was able to get a clear sight of his face, she let the leather bag she had been holding slip from her hand without even noticing. Her heart missed a beat and she almost fainted on the spot in shock. Never, for one moment, had she imagined that she would come across Wichai in the role of a major villain. It was the very same Wichai that had taken her away from Thepharat and then crushed her future into little pieces. She shut her eyes, unable to look. She only recovered when she heard a woman stop in front of the shop and call out to another woman who had emerged from the jewellery shop, telling her the awful thing that had happened.

'He's a real villain, he is. They say he's been making a living out of fleecing women for ages. Someone next door heard a girl crying for help, so they broke down the door. And what did they find? He was cutting his wife's throat with a razor! It's so awful. He wanted her gold belt and she wouldn't let him have it, so he killed her. Renting a room, they were, right here in the San Chao area.'

Reun shuddered. She had reconciled herself to her fate. Wichai was someone she wanted to forget completely. She did not hate him. All she wished for was that he were a thousand miles away, so that she would never ever see him again. And yet by chance she had come across him again under such horrifying circumstances. She had been lucky. If she had not given him what he wanted in the first place, he would surely have killed her. The bad karma he had created had turned full circle and rebounded upon him without the need for anyone to mete out punishment. Whether there was justice in the world or not, the divine and the hand of the law had performed their duty by reaching out and seizing the criminal by the throat.

Twenty

AFTER taking her daughter the pair of little red shoes and school bag she had asked for, Reun did not return to visit again for many days. She did not want her daughter to see her too often, because she felt she was unclean and she did not want to contaminate her innocent little child. When she missed her daughter, she would often go and watch her on her way to school, but always from a distance and making sure that she was out of sight. The sight of the sweet little girl filled her with joy; it strengthened her resolve to carry on working for the future happiness of her child and helped to keep her spirits up. Some days she earned a lot and then she would buy sweets, fruit, and presents and leave them at Mae Peu-ut's house. Just this was enough for this poor unfortunate mother.

When she was alone and had nothing to do, Reun would sit thinking. She thought of her child, who, with each day, was growing up into a young girl. As she grew up, Eet would doubtless begin to wonder about her mother. At first she would wonder why it was not possible for her to live with her mother like some of her friends. The other girls would talk about how their mothers loved them; how, in the morning, they would help them to get dressed and get ready for school, checking all their things; how, in the evening, they would fuss over their children's return from school and busy themselves getting a meal ready; and then, finally, when they were free, how they would caress their child lovingly. Eet's friends would say, 'My mummy's like this' or 'My mummy's like that' and Eet would just sit and listen sadly, because she had never been close to her mother like her friends. Eet's mother had never come and looked after her. On top of that, how upset she would have been if she had known that her own mother was neither a woman of some standing nor just an ordinary woman, like other children's mothers, but a prostitute, a whore, who made her living selling sex. It was so shameful. How could Eet ever face people? And worse, what if Eet's friends all despised her and looked down on her because she was the daughter of a prostitute? What would Eet do? The shame of having a prostitute for a mother would begin to gnaw away at her heart and weaken her resolve to study. Eventually, the child for whose happiness she had suffered every difficulty and hardship would simply begin to hate her mother.

Reun once again began to be affected by the words of two of her fellow patients in the hospital at the time when she was giving birth to Eet. They had spoken of a relative whose wife who had once been a prostitute. After the birth of her daughter, the woman had an affair, and there was a violent scene which ended with her having to leave the house with her daughter. It was this daughter that had prompted the woman in hospital to remark that she would come to no good like her mother, who was a prostitute. 'If you want to know the daughter,' she had said, quoting the old saying, 'look no further than her mother.' Reun brooded over what she had heard. While it was true that her heart was not tainted like her body, she could not help worrying that what had happened to her and her bad reputation would destroy Eet's future. No matter how beautiful, sweet-natured, polite, and dignified like her father she might be, no one would want to marry Eet, nor would they have any respect for her because of her mother's sins. No matter where she went, she would not be accepted. Where would Eet find any happiness?

When Reun stood before the large mirror and looked closely at herself, she felt sad. Carefully, she examined her hair, which had once grown thick and sleek but which now relied upon instruments of science to produce its wavy effect. Because she had her hair done so often, what had once been jet-black hair had become dry and brittle, with a reddish hue, and it had thinned out so that it no longer looked very attractive. Her face, which as a young girl had been full with a healthy pink glow to her cheeks, now appeared in the mirror full of wrinkles. Her cheeks were pale and hollow and her whole face was disfigured by dark spots. Her eyes which had once sparkled so brightly were dull and sunken with pain and sorrow. Her lips were pale and lifeless and she had become very thin, a mere bag of bones. Reun covered her face with make-up to mask the deterioration and make herself attractive to those she met as well as to reassure herself. But each time she saw herself in the mirror, it was like a Japanese picture that had been touched up with colour to attract the passer-by. When she began to perspire, the black make-up she had painted on her eyebrows began to run. Her complexion was uneven because of the cream and her lips were a mess. She sank down into a chair and sat there in despair. That was not her face and her body; rather, it was the face of a ghost.

Concern for her daughter and distress at her own appearance gradually led Reun to the conclusion that she should abandon her profession. At the same time, she needed advice on how to go about earning a living that would provide her with sufficient funds to support herself and her daughter. In the past, when she had needed advice, there had been Samorn to turn to. Now, there was no one who would have much real sympathy apart from Mae Choey, the owner of the house, who, she thought, was sensible enough to be able to offer some advice. So one day, while they were chatting, Reun took the opportunity to unburden herself.

'I'm so unhappy at the moment,' she confided, in a trembling voice. 'I want to get out of this kind of work. What do you think?'

Mae Choey looked at her and smiled. But underneath she was laughing at Reun. Many of her girls had come to her to say that they were fed-up and wanted to stop working but none of them ever succeeded. In fact, Reun was not of much use to her now as her looks had gone. In the daytime, there was no trace of freshness about her, and it was only at night, with the aid of make-up, that she looked passable. Mae Choey had many other girls who were better looking than Reun, certainly enough to support her for the future. Even if she lost Reun, it would not affect her income unduly. So what better than to agree with Reun and encourage her?

'It's good to be thinking along those lines. You're not looking in very good shape these days. It would be good to pack it in. This kind of work is for young girls. Once you start getting old, there's no money in it.'

'Yes, that's just what I've been thinking,' Reun replied sadly. 'That's why I want to get out.'

'You've only mentioned packing it in. What are you going to do instead? Or have you got someone who fancies you hidden away somewhere?' Mae Choey asked with a smile, thinking that her words would catch Reun on the raw.

'No, not at all,' Reun replied immediately. 'Whoever

would fancy me, looking like a barbecue stick? I was thinking that if I packed it in I'd go and rent a small room and sell
dried food. Just enough to get by on from day to day.'

'How could you rent a room all on your own?' Mae
Choey cried. 'It would be so lonely.'

'Oh, I'll manage. I'd take my kid to live with me to keep
me company,' Reun replied, her thoughts turning to her little
girl. If her plan worked out, she would be able to live with
her child without ever having to be parted again.

Mae Choey's expression turned to one of astonishment.
'What, you've got a kid then, have you? I didn't know that.
What is it, a boy or a girl?'

'A girl.'

'Ah, a girl. How old is she? Where's she living at the
moment?' Mae Choey enquired. Reun had been with her
for a long time, but it had never occurred to her that Reun
had a child. This was the first she had heard of it.

'She's getting on for five. I've been paying someone to
look after her ever since she was tiny. Now she lives in Bang
Krabeu.'

'Where's the father?' Mae Choey asked, looking at Reun.
'Or is he dead?'

Reun was prepared for Mae Choey's question. Reun was
a frank and honest person and she did not regard anything as
private, including personal details of her own life, even
though no one knew about it in any depth. In fact, Reun did
not want to talk about it any more, but since Mae Choey had
asked, she told her. 'He might be dead or he might be still
alive,' she said. 'My story is a bit different from the others,
you know. When I was younger, I lived at Ba Taht's. Do you
know her? She's from Phraeng Sanphasat.'

'Yes,' said Mae Choey. 'A fat woman with bulging eyes.'
From her manner it was clear that she was eager to hear
Reun's story.

'That's right. Well, I was there some time, and that's where I met my child's father.' Reun did not dare to tell Mae Choey Wit's name or much about him, because deep inside her she still wished to cherish his name. 'I loved him very much and kept myself just for him. Until I was two months pregnant....'

'Why did you let it go without doing anything about it?' Mae Choey interrupted.

The expression on Reun's face grew even sadder. Mae Choey's words reminded her of the day she had found out she was pregnant and Samorn had warned her to 'hurry up and sort it out right at the beginning'. If Reun had been cruel enough to discard that lump of flesh and blood that bore witness to the love between her and the man she worshipped, and do as she had been advised, there was no way of knowing how different her life might have been.

'Because I loved him,' Reun confessed. 'That's why I didn't do anything.'

'Did he know you were pregnant?' Mae Choey asked.

'No, he didn't know. Before I had a chance to tell him, he disappeared and never came back to see me again. Since then I've never set eyes on him.'

'Huh! What else do you expect from men,' Mae Choey sighed. 'It was a mistake to go falling in love. Why did you do it? He came for a bit of fun and then he lost interest. You should know well enough that people like us can't have love. It's just an exchange of wants—we want money and they want fun.'

Reun lowered her head in silence, leaving Mae Choey to ramble on. Most women who sell sex for a living feel much the same way as Mae Choey, but Reun had not felt that way at the beginning. It was necessity and fate which had made her a plaything for men. There was no need to sit revealing her innermost feelings to Mae Choey.

'Just look at me. In the fifteen years that I've been in the business, goodness knows how many men have said they loved me and asked me to go and live with them. But there's no way I would. Men are all the same, whether they're young or old. When they want money, you have to go off and pawn whatever you've got and then come running back with the money for them. Once you're broke, they get bored. You have a bit of a row and then they start knocking you about and going off with other women. Don't go wasting your time on men. It's better making a living this way. Who cares if it's tough? No one's going to take your things away and you don't have to worry about anyone else.'

Of course, Mae Choey thought it was a good way of making a living and did not care how tough it was. After all, she did not work any more. All she did was sit there waiting to welcome customers. But Reun had to endure the pain of earning her money herself; and instead of spending what she earned just on herself, she had to share it with Mae Choey and her own child. There was a vast difference in the kind of hardship experienced by the two women.

'You and I are different, though,' Reun replied, not wanting to contradict Mae Choey. 'I've got a child to worry about. It's not so convenient doing this kind of work.'

'Selling things isn't a bad idea,' said Mae Choey, 'but you've got to have capital. At least you don't need any for what we're selling at the moment, though,' she added with a laugh.

'The thought of how I'm going to get some money together really depresses me. Do you know anyone who would lend me a bit?' Reun's expression reflected her anxiety.

'It's difficult, you know, Reun,' said Mae Choey, looking thoughtful. 'There are plenty of people who will lend money, but they want some kind of surety and we haven't got anything to offer them. Then there's the Indian fellow, Ban

Singh, whom you've borrowed money from before. He doesn't come any more and he charges a lot of interest.'

'What about the landlord of this house? People say he's rich. Would you do me a favour and borrow some for me? I don't need very much. I think 50 baht would be enough.'

Mae Choey was silent for a while. Then she nodded, although she knew it would be in vain. 'All right, I'll have a word with him. But I don't think it'll do any good.'

Mae Choey's reply offered little hope, but even so, Reun waited in hope each day for word from Mae Choey. Slowly, her hopes dissolved, because people like Mae Choey really never have any thoughts of helping anyone. After saying she would help, she seemed to just forget about it; and when she was reminded, she um-ed and ah-ed her way out.

All hope now gone and with no plans, Reun sank deeper into depression. She missed her child. She wanted her little girl to be happy and she wanted to be near her, but it was impossible. Whatever plans she thought up, they never came to fruition. She became more and more depressed and grew thinner and thinner. Whenever she closed her eyes, all she saw was her little daughter's face floating around in front of her, gazing at her as if she was crying out for her protection. Her dearest Eet. She had never intended to abandon her to someone else. She desperately wanted her child to be with her, but she had no idea what to do about it. Her daughter would blame her for treating her own child so cruelly. She had to admit it because it was true. It was quite right. She was cruel. Cruel for not providing happiness and prosperity for her child. She kept her sorrow to herself and then turned her thoughts once again to what Samorn had said just before she died. Samorn had wanted her to have a husband who would give her security. She had not wanted Reun to go on work-ing this way. But had Reun done as she had promised?

Reun's body could not stand up to the damage her spirits

had suffered and her health began to deteriorate. She would
be all right for three days and then on the fourth she would
have a fever. Her symptoms were like Samorn's: she had a dry
cough, she had gone very thin, and her heart was gradually
getting weaker. It was as if she was living just to see one last
hope realized: the hope of seeing Wit, so that she could leave
her child in his care. However, none of Reun's hopes had
ever come to anything. Always they remained unfulfilled,
unattainable, so that she scarcely any longer wanted anything
from life, apart from the most real of all things—the last
breath of life.

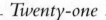

Twenty-one

THE taxi slowly drew up in the pouring rain alongside the
pavement on Ratchadamnoen Avenue. The electric lights
shining from the branches of the mahogany trees made it
possible to see some young men dressed in suits getting out
of the vehicle one by one. The fourth and last one took out a
1-baht note and gave it to the driver and then hurried off
through the rain after his friends. They were standing in front
of the gate of a rather old two-storey house that had been
painted light blue. He gathered his grey raincoat tightly
around him and peered up. 'What are you still waiting out
here for?' he asked.

'What do you mean, "waiting"?' retorted one sharply.
'Khun Samarn's knocked three times and there's no answer.'

'All right, there's no need to go losing your temper, now.
We're supposed to be having a good time. Perhaps, with all
that rain beating down on the roof, Khun Samarn didn't knock
loudly enough. Let me have a go.' The man who had just
joined his friends banged again loudly so that his hand hurt.

'All right, I heard you,' a voice shouted in reply.

From inside came the sound of wooden clogs running to unbolt the door. The door was thrown open and without waiting to see who had opened it, the young men not wearing raincoats rushed in, leaving their companion to bring up the rear. He smiled gratefully at the young girl who had opened the door and went upstairs. He removed his soaking shoes, placed them in a row next to those of his three companions, and then went into the living-room where they had hung their jackets up to dry and were now sitting cheerfully. Once inside, his companions, being familiar with the place, introduced him to the owner with the words, 'Here's a new visitor. He's never been here before.'

The owner rose to greet him with a smile. 'Let me take your raincoat.'

'Don't worry. I'll just hang it over this chair,' the newcomer said, smiling pleasantly and shaking his coat vigorously before spreading it over the nearest chair. He bent over and brushed the rain from his French silk jacket and brown silk trousers and then went and sat with his companions. He looked at the owner and the three girls who had joined his friends and were now laughing and joking in an intimate fashion, just as they were required to do and as they had done on previous occasions.

Mae Choey, the owner, saw him sitting quietly on his own, not taking any interest in any of the girls. 'You must work in the same department as Tan Khun, I suppose,' she said. She was referring to the tall, thin man of about forty who looked older than the other men and who, at that moment, was chatting intimately with one of the girls.

'Yes,' he replied briefly.

'You look as if you don't go out at night very much,' she said with a smile, secretly admiring his handsome face. He was more serious and more polite than his companions.

'No, not very much,' he said with a good-humoured laugh. 'I used to, for a while, but then I stopped. It must have been five or six years ago. We've just been to the Ratchawong area and my friends dragged me along.'

'What's all this you're saying about me?' Khun Samarn called out after overhearing them.

'Oh, nothing. Nothing at all,' Mae Choey hurriedly reassured him. 'Your friend was just telling me that he had to come because his friends invited him and he hadn't really intended to come along himself tonight.'

Everyone laughed. But while everyone downstairs was enjoying themselves, upstairs the unfortunate Reun stood leaning against the window, gazing outside at the rain as it poured down in large drops. It was cool because of the rain, just as it had been that night when it had rained six years ago. That night when Wit had gone to see her at Phraeng Sanphasat. It was just like that night and there were even flashes of lightning again, too. She remembered everything so distinctly. Wit's words, his manner, even his tone of voice that day, she recalled so vividly. He had tried to comfort her when he had realized how unhappy she was. He had told her not to blame herself for being a prostitute and she had slept soundly, locked in his embrace.

She realized that now, as she waited forlorn to tell Wit the truth about the little child, he would probably have forgotten all about his faithful Reun. He would surely have another girl clinging to his side and another child, who would be his pride and joy, to match his status. She was unaware of the tears streaming down her face. Reun had seen the four young men get out of the taxi and dash through the pouring rain towards the house. As she watched, her thoughts had gone back to the day when she had seen Wit off at the door and he had put a necklace around her neck. He had been so sad when he left. Wit loved her. He had promised to take her as his wife. But why had he left her? Left her and never returned.

The sound of laughter downstairs grew louder, prompting Reun to quickly dry her eyes. Mae Choey had several visitors. She had better go down and see if she wanted her to fetch anything. For the last two or three days, she had not been of much use here, apart from doing Mae Choey's laundry. She powdered her tear-stained face, combed her hair, and went downstairs. On her way down, Mae Choey called out, 'Whoever that is walking about, could you fetch a glass of water, please?'

Reun took a glass out of the small cupboard and filled it with water from the jug by the wall. She put the glass on an aluminium tray and carried it into the living room. Everyone was chatting away and no one took any notice of her except the man who was sitting talking with Mae Choey. He looked up and stared straight at Reun. When she saw his face, she dropped the tray and glass in shock. The glass shattered into little pieces when it hit the ground. Before the others even had time to look round in surprise, Reun had quickly bent down and begun to pick up the pieces of glass. Her heart was pounding so loudly it was almost audible.

'How on earth did you manage to drop it?' Mae Choey scolded her. 'You'd better make sure you clear it all up. Otherwise someone's going to get cut.'

'If a glass doesn't break when it's dropped, it's not much of a glass,' one of the men joked.

'Thank you very much, Khun Rote,' Mae Choey said, fixing him with a look of disapproval.

When it was apparent that only one glass was broken and that the person responsible was clearing up the mess, everyone returned to their conversations. When she had thrown away the broken pieces, Reun brought in a fresh glass of water and took it to the man, her hand visibly trembling.

'You don't seem too well,' he said, looking at her. 'You should rest. If you come down when you're not well, you'll only get worse.'

It really was her Wit. His face and voice had not changed at all. Reun was on the point of throwing herself down on his lap as she had before and telling him that here was Reun, his Reun. Tears of happiness welled up in her eyes. She scarcely dared answer, simply gazing back at him with a mixture of hope, excitement, and joy. She slipped away and sat out of sight in a dimly lit room from where she could see his face clearly. It was the face of a man in his thirties, grave and well-mannered, with bushy eyebrows over his bold eyes, thin lips, and clean-shaven around his cheeks and chin. She squeezed her hands tightly as she sat waiting for a suitable chance to see him alone. 'That, my sweet child,' she thought to herself, 'is my last hope of giving you happiness.'

Wit had not recognized Reun because she had changed so much. She was no longer beautiful and attractive as she had been when he had left her. But having noticed the way the sad-looking woman had entered the room and her shock—to the point of dropping the glass—when she saw him, Wit began to wonder. Her face was so pale, like that of someone with no strength. He waited until Mae Choey had finished speaking and then politely excused himself. He went into the badly lit room and stood in front of her in the dim light.

Reun had watched him glance over in her direction and then get up and walk towards her until he was standing there, right before her. He was even touching her shoulder. Reun trembled with joy. 'Aren't you feeling well?' she heard him ask gently. Her Wit. Was it really possible that he did not recognize her? Trying hard to keep her pounding heart under control, she looked up and asked in a trembling voice, 'Khun Wit, don't you remember me?'

He was puzzled that this pale-looking woman should know his name, but he laughed good-humouredly. 'You mean this place? Five or six years ago, I used to go out a bit, that's true, but it's not something that stuck in my memory. After all, every day one has to go here or there to goodness knows how many places, especially when one is a man. The truth is, I have to tell you I don't remember everyone I've met, nor where I went, nor what I did several years ago.'

Reun was silent for some while. Then feeling hurt, she said, 'Since you think you can't remember me because you were never really interested, I don't want to bring up the past to trouble you or disturb your happiness. But necessity forces me to speak because once your path crossed mine.'

Wit looked at the woman sitting before him in amazement. 'You say my path crossed yours?' he cried.

'Khun Wit, do you still remember Reun?' she asked with a lump in her throat.

Wit was silent for a moment before he replied. 'I think I do,' he said, leaning forward and staring at her suspiciously. 'Why, what have you got to do with Reun?'

The more she heard questions like this, the sadder Reun felt. 'Nothing,' she replied. 'I don't have anything to do with Reun, because she and I are one and the same person. Khun Wit, please use your eyes properly and look at me again clearly.'

Wit was shocked. He looked her up and down closely. 'Reun, is it really you? You've changed so much. You've changed and you look terrible now. I wouldn't have thought it possible.'

Tears flowed down Reun's cheeks in response. She covered her face with her hands and sobbed. Wit stood there, as if rooted to the ground. His thoughts went back to that time and poor Reun and all that had been between them.

'Necessity forces me to speak because once your path crossed mine,' were the words she had used. It was true. As a carefree young man, he had indeed become involved with this poor woman, who had once been so lovely, with frank, sparkling eyes, and who was now so pale and thin. He remembered. He remembered all about her past. He remembered his promise to take her away and go and live together as husband and wife. He had never dreamed that after leaving her that day he would ever see her again. She was crying and sobbing. This was not the sign of someone trying to trick him; Reun had always been an honest girl. It had been six years ago and even though she was doubtless hurt that he had not been to see her, nor kept his promise, she surely would not deceive him for the sake of gain. He pulled up a chair and sat down close to her, touching her gently on the arm to comfort her. 'You must have been very deeply hurt, Reun,' he said, 'that after promising to take you away from that kind of life, I just disappeared and never returned even once. I'll tell you everything, right from the beginning. Not as an excuse, because trying to make excuses wouldn't benefit either you or me.'

'Yes, you're absolutely right,' Reun said. 'Making excuses to a prostitute like me wouldn't benefit either you or me.' The hurt was quite apparent in her voice.

Wit looked into Reun's face. 'You're angry with me,' he said. 'But when you've heard what I have to say, you'll see that I didn't just sit back and do nothing about the promise I had made. In the beginning, I did everything I could to find a job so that I could take you to live with me. But I didn't have any success. My mother was most unhappy about what I wanted to do. Then she sent me to the Philippines for further study which would be beneficial to my future. I was going to tell you on that last day when we saw each other, but I was afraid you'd be so upset. It's a common mistake among men when they're young and carefree. You still know very little about life, Reun. If you had studied and known more about it, you would forgive me and not be angry with me. Everything is changing all the time; nothing ever stays the same.'

'No one was to blame. Youth, foolishness, and some strange invisible power led me to believe that I loved you, even though I wasn't certain whether I was right in what I was doing. In the end, however, I was sent abroad to the Philippines. At first I wanted to tell you how much I missed you. I felt that my family had sent me abroad, not out of any high hopes, but so as to torture me to death. In actual fact, it couldn't have been any other way. Leaving aside my future, if I hadn't been sent to the Philippines, then we might have lived together, just the two of us. No one could have stopped us if that was what we wanted. Now, having received a better education, I feel that the way I had behaved was extremely selfish. I should use that good education to benefit the public, my family, and myself. Isn't that so, Reun? Love can fade away. It can change, but the goodness that is in love and which depends on love for comfort is greater.' He paused for a moment and then continued. 'I was in the Philippines for four years. I struggled in my own way just as you struggled and changed. Everyone's life is different. You and I have gone through different joys and sorrows. Don't have regrets about the powers beyond us which condemn everyone this way. I myself cannot say any more than this what made me change. I'm married now, Reun. I'm not the same Wit who used to love you in that carefree way. Our surroundings which are necessary for our lives force us all to commit sins and to face sin with courage. The weak are victims of sin and they can never feel pure in their hearts until they have paid the debt for their sin. Reun, please sacrifice your own feelings and be happy for me, now that I am married and have been for six months.'

Twenty-two

REUN felt a piercing pain in her heart as she sat listening to Wit. She parted her lips and then pressed them together tightly. 'I'm happy that you're married and have set up home,' she said slowly in a sad voice. Wit stared at her. But there was no trace of cunning or pretence in her eyes. She was so honest and so pitiful.

'Even if you hadn't told me about the circumstances which made it impossible for you to keep your promises, I still wouldn't be angry, because I always knew our backgrounds were so different. Even at the very beginning, when you said you'd help me, I pointed out that you were from a high-ranking family and that you were still young and shouldn't go getting involved with an ordinary worthless prostitute like me. Isn't that what I said?' Seeing Wit nod in agreement, she continued, the resentment that any woman in her position would feel flashing in her eyes. 'Those words are witness that I feel no sorrow that powers beyond us condemned us to change. You have gained education and advancement in your life, while I have had to struggle so hard in mine. Now that I've met you again tonight, I have no desire to cause you any trouble by bringing up the past, or to ask for your pity or to remember what was once between us. All I want to do is to tell you that I have waited a long time to be able to ask you for some help. Not for myself,' she said, her voice almost dropping to a whisper, 'but for your child, Wit, your child whom I bore.'

When he heard this, Wit stared at Reun in amazement. Anyone else would have looked shocked and denied it instantly if a prostitute had come along and claimed she had borne his child. Wit controlled any such impulse and simply cried out, 'My child!'

Reun saw quite clearly the look of doubt on his face. 'Yes, your child,' she repeated. 'Perhaps you don't believe it's true, but I beg you to listen to me first. Since you do remember me, you must remember me and all the others at Ba Taht's house saying that after I met you, I wouldn't go with anyone else. Do you remember?' she asked putting her hand over her mouth as she coughed two or three times.

Wit was silent and then nodded. 'Yes, I remember something like that. But that was only because you loved me, wasn't it?' There were still signs of doubt on his face.

Reun gave a forced laugh. 'It's not a case of just because I loved you. My love for you had consequences. That was when I got pregnant. I was going to tell you the last day you came to see me, but I didn't like to because I could see you weren't well. I thought I'd tell you another day. But that turned out to be no more than a hope and you never came to see me again until tonight. I want you to know that I have raised and supported the child until now. My strength is gone. I've done my duty. From now on, please accept and look after the child as your responsibility.'

Wit looked tense. He laughed loudly. 'What you've just told me sounds like some fairy-tale,' he said harshly.

'It's not funny, Khun Wit,' Reun said, staring at him bitterly. 'You may not want to accept that you're the father, but let me assure you again that I have no wish to deceive you in the hope of getting something out of you. I'm a prostitute, and that's the way I have to struggle on. I don't want to use the child to tie you to me, nor have you look after the child if you don't accept it. I'd rather just struggle on and bring her up on my own. Why should hardship worry me, after all I've been through, driving myself almost into the grave for my only child? In fact, I'm actually proud that even though I'm a prostitute, a whore, despised by the whole world, I have still laid down and used my sordid life to bring into the world and raise the flesh and blood of a highly honoured man, providing for its happiness, upbringing, and education.'

Reun paused and coughed two or three times. 'But how much longer I can support her from my sordid living, I don't know,' she said pressing her hand against her throat. 'The human body is unpredictable. All I'm afraid of is that without me, the child will suffer because there'll be no one to look after her. She will reap the karma without knowing of the actions of those who brought her into the world. Something you never expected to happen has happened. Yes, it's true you're a man with a position of prestige and honour, and people treat you with respect wherever you go. But there is one woman, not a respectable one, but a prostitute, who knows very well that you are not an honourable man, and that you have no humanity when you refuse to take responsibility for your own flesh and blood. You said that our surroundings, which are necessary for our lives, force us all to commit sins and to face sin with courage, and that the weak are victims of sin and can never feel pure in their hearts until they have paid the debt for their sin. Let me point out that you are condemned by your very own words because you're a man who dares not face up to his sins and you have not repaid the debt on the sins you have committed. What about me? I have a clear conscience for having endured a life of prostitution. I've totally accepted my fate as a payment for my sins.'

Reun paused, weak and breathless. She was not very good with words, but what she had been through had taught her to say what she really felt and what lay at the bottom of her heart. It was these very words which gradually softened Wit's hardened heart so that he believed her and took pity on her.

'What's the point of life? Is it just so we can be good?' Reun cried, laughing wildly. 'What kind of morality is it when a little child's life is tossed aside like a stone? What good does it do when people believe that the father's blood is better than the mother's? The father's blood gives the child rank and family. So much for the blood of gentlefolk. Where is their morality?' Her voice dropped to a barely audible mumble. 'My darling little child, my only child, you're better off with a prostitute for a mother than going around saying you're from a high-class family on your father's side. I may be only a woman, but I will care for you until the very last drop of blood has gone from my body.'

She turned to Wit, her face full of sadness and bitterness. He remained silent, his head bowed like someone contemplating some wrong they have committed. A feeling of tenderness drew Reun to him and she threw herself down at his feet. 'My darling,' she moaned, 'let me call you that just one more time. I should have killed myself long ago, you know, but I'm not dead yet. I've waited to see you to tell you about the child. Khun Wit, even though I don't like what you've done, I still love you. I love you, but without wanting anything from you.'

Wit bent over and helped Reun up. 'No, Reun,' he said in a trembling voice. 'Don't do that. It was bad enough when you were cursing me. Don't make it even more painful. Forgive me if I seemed not to believe you. I believe you now. I really do believe that I am the father of your child. Reun, stop crying and look at me and just see whether or not I'm pleased with the news.'

Reun did as Wit asked her. She looked up and saw him smiling. Tears welled up in her eyes again; but this time they were tears of joy and hope.

'I'm grateful to you,' said Wit, 'and I really sympathize with you for all your efforts in bringing the child up, amid all the hardship and at the cost of your health.'

Reun forced a smile. She had followed the path of prostitution to earn the money to raise her child and now all she got was 'I'm grateful to you and I really sympathize with you', was it?

'I didn't bring her up in the hope of gaining your gratitude,' she said. 'I did it because I felt it was my duty.'

Wit was shamed into silence. Eventually, he reached out and squeezed her thin, ice-cold hand. 'All right, Reun. Your heavy burden is gone now. I'm going to accept my responsibilities from now on. But you haven't told me yet where our child is. Does she live here with you?'

'No, I don't look after her myself. It wouldn't have been proper, me living with my daughter with my job and reputation. I didn't want people to gossip and point at her and say she'd end up a prostitute like her mother when she grew up. That's why I paid a couple to look after her for me, ever since she was tiny.'

'My child is a girl,' said Wit, 'and you've paid someone else to raise her? I hope they're a couple you can really trust. What kind of people are they?'

'At first I didn't really trust them, because they weren't very straight with me. They often overcharged me for milk and looking after the baby. I was well aware of it but I didn't say anything. It's a normal thing for people who haven't got very much. They tend to be selfish over little things, but I couldn't find anyone else apart from them. Now Eet, that's her name—I was calling her that temporarily—has grown up with them and loves them as if she were their real daughter.'

'Where's their house?' Wit asked anxiously. 'Would it be difficult for you if I asked you to take me to see the child now? I can hardly wait to see her.'

'Last month they set up a fruit stall in Bang Krabeu,' Reun replied. ' But it didn't do very well, so they packed up and went and rented a house in Trork Wat Tri by Banglampu Bridge. Would it be difficult for me to take you there? It's up to you.'

Wit got up and gently squeezed the top of Reun's arm. 'Let's go now, then.' He walked out of the room and into the living-room, ignoring his friends, who turned and stared after him. He took 10 baht from his jacket pocket and gave it to Mae Choey, telling her he wanted to take Reun out.

'Of course, if you want to,' said Mae Choey, granting her permission and accepting his money. 'I've got no objections.' But underneath she was astonished that a young man like Wit should go for Reun, who was getting on a bit and looked pale and sickly. She had lots of other attractive young girls, but Wit had not seemed interested.

Tan Khun heard Wit quite clearly. 'Eh, what's up with Wit today, then?' he complained to a friend, loud enough for Wit to hear. 'What's he going off on his own for? I've never seen him acting this strangely before,' he added, casting a disdainful look in the direction of Reun, who was standing waiting for Wit by the door.

'Oh that's up to him,' a friend whispered. ' Why should it be so surprising? Maybe they hit it off together. You look down on her, Khun Samarn. She's not good-looking but she might be all right underneath.'

Wit ignored the teasing. He waved goodbye to his companions, picked up his raincoat, put on his hat, and followed Reun out of the house. Outside, it was still drizzling. The path was dimly visible by the light from the upstairs room. He flagged down a taxi and opened the door for Reun to get in first. Once he had sat down, he told the driver to go to Banglampu.

It was cold as the taxi sped on its way. Seeing that Reun was unwell and coughing a lot, Wit gave her his raincoat to wrap around her. Neither spoke during the journey. Reun huddled up against the back of the seat and remained silent until the car crossed Norarat Bridge and came to a small lane. She dragged herself out of the corner and told the driver to stop at the top of the lane. Wit opened the door and jumped out first. As he helped Reun out, he instructed the driver to wait. Then they walked down the dark, unlit lane.

It was still drizzling. The lane was wide enough for a car but it was pitted with waterlogged holes. Even on foot it was easy to stumble, and Wit offered Reun his hand for fear that she might trip and fall. About half-way down, Reun led Wit off to the left, past a Chinese coffee-shop and into a narrow lane that was only wide enough to walk in single file. On the right was a corrugated iron fence which they used to help balance themselves. Wit grumbled about the smell of rotting garbage along the way and cursed when he stepped on a muddy patch. Reun made no complaint other than coughing two or three times because of the cold air. She pulled Wit's raincoat tightly around her. They passed a house where the occupants were still up. They had lit a lantern and there were several people sitting around chatting. Clearly visible from the light was a row of wooden houses to the left with corrugated iron roofs. Reun led Wit up to the fifth house which was the only one where the door was still open. The couple who lived there had not yet gone to bed and were sitting together chatting. Reun stopped and turned to Wit. 'This is the house,' she said.

Hearing a woman's voice and someone stopping in front of his house, Nai Klin picked up a *pakaoma* and tied it round the old batik sarong he was wearing. He picked up the lantern and shone it outside. 'Oh, Reun. It's you. What are you doing, coming so late? Besides, it's raining.' As he greeted her, he was startled to see a man of smart appearance with her. 'Do come in,' he said. 'Reun, bring the gentleman in.' He turned and went inside and put the lantern down. As he searched around for a shirt, he whispered to Mae Peu-ut, who was standing there awkwardly, that Reun had brought a strange man along with her.

Wit took a deep breath and followed Reun inside. The room was a mess and the owners clearly took little interest in keeping things tidy. Two old mosquito nets had already been set up, using old rags tied to the corners. The walls were covered in old newspapers and there was a shelf with a Buddha image on it above a clothes rail. Standing against the wall was an assortment of crockery and utensils, including jars, betel bowls, and bottles. As he sat down, Wit's gaze came to rest on a pair of red leather shoes that were neither new nor old, which had been placed by the wall near the door. 'Please don't bother,' he said to the couple as they fussed about, fetching him a drink and a mat to sit on. 'I've come about a certain matter and I'll be leaving shortly,' he added, looking at Reun as if to say, 'Where is she, then?'

Reun turned to Mae Peu-ut and Nai Klin. 'He wanted to come and see Eet,' she said.

'Eet's asleep,' they replied in unison, looking first at Wit and then at Reun. 'She's just gone to sleep. If you like, you can go in and have a look. She's in that mosquito net—the one over there,' Nai Klin added, pointing to the large net which had been set up on the other side of the red floral curtain which divided the room. 'Reun, go and take the gentleman to have a look.'

Reun did as he suggested. She picked up the lantern, looked at Wit, and then led the way. She ducked under the net strings, went behind the curtain, and knelt down in front of the large, heavily patched, and rather grubby net. With her left hand, she raised the end of the net sufficiently to reveal the figure of a little girl fast asleep on a small, old, red mattress. Her head was no longer resting on the pillow and she lay with her hands sprawled out, naked under the old tattered blanket which half-covered her. Wit felt his heart pounding as he peered in to look at his child. He gazed down at the pale, smooth face, amazed at the similarity between her

features and his own. As he looked down at the slim figure
stretched out on the mattress, his gaze fell upon her necklace.
He recognized it quite clearly as the one he had given Reun
on the day he had left her. There could no longer be any
doubt, nor any grounds for him to suspect that Reun was
trying to deceive him. He was quite convinced that this tiny
girl with the sweet little face lying fast asleep before him was
really his own flesh and blood, who had come into the world
unknown to him. The bond between father and child drew
him closer and with trembling hands he reached out and
touched her fine hair. Filled with emotion, he looked once
again at her face. He heaved a deep sigh which Reun heard
clearly. Then, slowly, he got up and returned to where the
husband and wife were sitting. Wit's face dropped. A feeling
of pity that his little child should have to live in such a place
left him numb and speechless. It was only when Reun came
and sat down beside him that he pulled himself together.

Twenty-three

At the command of one of the passengers, the taxi which
had stood waiting at the top of Trork Wat Tri Thotsathep
drove back to Ratchadamnoen Avenue. The rain had stopped
now, leaving the air cool and fresh. Wit and Reun both sat in
silence, as they had on the way out, neither uttering a word.
It was only their inner feelings that differed. For Wit, the
shock of seeing his child had now given way to a feeling of
love and protectiveness, as he sat there in the car. In his
mind's eye, he could still see the child's face and eyes. As a
young man born into a wealthy family, he had hardly ever
encountered poverty. When he saw his child in a dirty room
and in surroundings that would only damage her health and

development, it made him feel even more pity for her. But for Reun, there was nothing strange about poverty because it was something she had experienced. What she did feel at this moment was a sense of excitement and happiness that her wish, her ultimate hope, was to be fulfilled and a pleasant feeling of warmth at sitting next to the father of her child, the man who had once been hers, but now belonged to another woman. It was this that made her reflective on the journey home.

When the car drew up, Wit got out and told the driver to wait. 'Why aren't you going straight home?' Reun asked quietly as she rose from her seat.

'There's one other small matter concerning the child that I wanted to talk to you about,' Wit replied as he helped her from the car. He followed her and they stopped in the shadows of the doorway. He told her not to knock on the door. 'Here will do, Reun. There's no need to go in. My friends will all have gone by now.' He peered into the house. The light was still on and there were muffled voices coming from inside, from another party, he presumed. He turned to Reun who stood resting against the corrugated iron doorway. There was silence for a moment before he spoke.

'Reun, I feel so sorry for my child having to live like that. That doesn't mean I'm blaming you for causing her hardship. It's rather that I feel, like you said, that I haven't repaid my debt. I can't begin to compare myself with all that you've been through as a woman. From now on, it's my duty to provide for the child, and for you, too, Reun. I intend to find a place for you to live with the child.'

Wit scarcely had time to finish before Reun objected. 'No, Wit, no,' she sobbed. 'I don't want to live with my child. It's not that I don't love her. I tell you in all sincerity that I want to be close to her. But I can't simply do as I want, because I know that if I did, it wouldn't do her any good. My reputation is permanently tarnished, and it will affect my daughter, too. Besides, people will say that the mother of your child is a prostitute and that your mistress is a prostitute and you're renting a house for her. Please take the child and bring her up on her own. Don't bother about me. You're no longer single like you were. You've got a wife and it's your duty to be honest and straight with her and to look after and provide for her and her family. If you were to go to the extent of renting a house for me and providing money for us to live on, it would be like me sharing the same rights as your wife. I couldn't do that.'

'I'm sorry if you won't let me have the chance to repay some of your goodness,' said Wit. 'As far as the child is concerned, that's agreed. I'll take her to live with me. But you'll have to give me another two or three days, because I'll have to have a word with Jitra first.' The thought of breaking the news about his child to Jitra, his wife, weighed heavily on his mind.

Reun quickly suppressed the hurt she felt when Wit mentioned his wife's name. 'I'm really afraid that all this about me and the child is going to upset Khun Jitra, because I know just how a woman feels. She might hate the child.'

'I'm sure it won't be that way, Reun,' Wit countered. 'You've not met Jitra. She's a well-educated woman. She's a quiet, gentle person and I've noticed she loves children, too.'

'I didn't mean that Khun Jitra would be jealous or resentful of the child. What I was talking about was the hurt she will feel when she learns that you have had a child with a prostitute like me. Even if she is well-educated, no matter how calm and detached a person she might be, she can't help but feel saddened to see her husband's child borne by another woman and not herself. Every woman wants a faithful husband and a family life where there is one husband and one wife. If such wishes are not fulfilled, it causes suffering and this will spread to you and, eventually, the child, which means three lives altogether. Any hopes of a happy, married life together would dissolve in bitterness and sorrow. Just think very carefully what it would mean.'

'I agree with what you say,' said Wit. 'But what can I do? If what has happened causes such sorrow, it is because of powers that are beyond us. Everyone is condemned to pay their debt in life, and to be the victim of sin. People have to accept their fate and pay off the debt of their sins. It is the only way we can save ourselves from falling under such powers. We must shake off all feelings that lead to despair and grasp our humanitarian responsibilities. Everyone has to sacrifice some of their rights in order to preserve their remaining rights. That's what Jitra will have to do. That's settled then, Reun. The child will be happy and well-looked after in my care. I'll send news in a couple of days.' As he spoke, he fumbled in his jacket pocket for an envelope containing money.

'You don't have to hurry,' Reun replied, hugging herself to keep warm. 'I'd rather the situation with Jitra is sorted out first.'

'In that case, I'll come back here again next Saturday night. In the meantime, take this, because it'll be several days before we meet again.' He handed her 50 baht, which was virtually all he had with him, keeping only sufficient for the taxi.

'No, there's no need,' said Reun, refusing the money. 'I don't want anything from you at all. By agreeing to bring up our daughter, you have made me quite happy enough.'

But Wit insisted. 'Take it, Reun,' he said sadly. 'Don't think too much about it. I've heard you coughing. Get some medicine with it.' With his free hand, he took Reun's hand and drew her closer to him, but Reun pulled her hand away.

'I'm all right,' she replied, trying to keep a steady voice. 'I've just got a bit of a cough. It'll soon be better. I don't want any money from you. That would look as if I had brought my child up in the hope of getting something in return. There's nothing between us anymore. Do you understand?'

Wit persisted. 'If you won't take it for yourself, then please take it for the child. I'm giving you the money for the child.' This ploy was more successful and Reun held out her hand to accept the money. He squeezed her hand tightly and gazed at her with a strange look in his eye. It was not the way a young man might look at the girl he loved but rather how an older brother might look at his younger sister.

Reun stood staring in a daze after Wit until the taxi had disappeared from sight. She returned to the house and as soon as she went into the living-room where two of the girls were sitting with Mae Choey, they began to tease her. 'What's all this, then, Reun?' one of the girls greeted her, clearing her throat as she spoke. 'How come you're back so soon? I thought it'd be tomorrow morning before you'd be home. You were certainly the leading lady tonight.'

'Tonight's star was certainly in luck,' said the second girl, continuing with the leg-pulling. 'Having a leading man as fine and good-looking as a little god, and loaded, too. Why don't we ever have such luck?'

Suffering and poor health had left Reun ill-humoured. No one was going to be sarcastic to her. She was about to shout and curse them but managed to control herself, realizing that it was only normal for girls to tease their friends in this manner. It was especially the case among those who made a living this way. Reun simply turned and walked away out of the room and up the stairs. From there she could just make out Mae Choey's voice. 'I don't know what the matter is with Reun,' she complained. 'She's so unpredictable. One minute she's chatting away with you ever so nicely, and then the next, she's sitting there moping. If you try to get involved, it will just drive you round the bend.'

Reun took off her jacket and hung it over the rail. She went over to the window and stood gazing out aimlessly. The excitement, the hope, and the sorrow of the day's events had forced her mind to work overtime. It was the excitement and hope at meeting Wit, the only man she had ever really loved, after being separated for five or six years. She was so pleased to see him. Even his voice was still kind and gentle. But his manner towards Reun was not that of the Wit of old. She pursed her lips with a feeling of sadness. Why hadn't he put his arms around her? Perhaps because she was a prostitute. But even then she had been. Or perhaps it was because his circumstances had changed, because he had been married for six months. Wit's words that evening still echoed in her ears: 'Please sacrifice your own feelings and be happy for me, now that I am married.' Once he used to whisper words of love to her; he would go on and on about how much he cared for her. But such behaviour, he now claimed, was common among young men full of high spirits and lacking in judgement. He had loved Reun for the wrong reasons; he had been carried away by foolish infatuation.

'Khun Wit,' Reun mumbled incoherently, unaware of the words that periodically escaped from her lips. 'You don't have to ask me to sacrifice my own feelings because I don't have enough feelings for you to sacrifice. Our lives are different. You are a man of flawless reputation from a large and prominent family and you have a wife of impeccable virtue. All this is far removed from a prostitute like me. But I've never wanted to hold you back. Let me congratulate you on having a wife. Jitra—it's an attractive name. Jitra ... Jitra—it shows she's got class.'

Reun became conscious of the draught coming from the window. She felt the chill pierce her heart. She turned away, switched off the electric light, and prepared for bed. As she lay down, she opened her eyes and gazed up at the top of the mosquito net. There she saw an image of her child, floating right before her eyes. She closed her eyes but her child's face would not go away. It was as if Eet was putting up a fierce struggle and refusing to go with her father. Reun started suddenly and opened her eyes. She began to think again. The thought of her dear little Eet made her feel she wanted to look after the child herself. She did not want her child to be parted from her and taken to live under the care of an adoptive mother. Jitra … it was a nice name, but whether or not she would love the child like a mother, Reun had no way of knowing. Before long, Jitra would have a child of her own. Then what would happen to Eet, who everyone knew had a prostitute for a mother? She would just be neglected and ignored. No one would take any interest in her. Her father would forget her and go and fuss over his new child by the woman he loved for the right reasons. Whenever Eet did anything wrong, they would curse and beat her and show none of the feelings towards her that a mother has for her child. 'I'm not giving you my child,' Reun cried out loudly. 'I'm not giving her to you.'

When she returned to her senses, Reun began to think about her own condition. 'I don't know how long I'm going to be able to take care of you, 'she mumbled sadly. 'I'm dying, you know.' She twisted at the pain in her heart. Her body hurt all over. 'I shall die without having been able to see to your future happiness,' she continued in delirium. 'My soul won't rest once I've gone. You'll blame me for making your life difficult and … Mae Peu-ut and Nai Klin looked after you well because I paid them. They don't love you as much as I do. They would never have dreamed of sacrificing everything for you. When I die, that'll be the end of their money and their interest. So who else can you go and live with, apart from your father?'

With these thoughts running through her mind, she suddenly opened the mosquito net and went and switched the light on. She dragged her body over to the dressing-table which stood next to a wardrobe with a full-length mirror. She steadied herself against the mirror frame and looked closely at herself, just as she always had whenever she had thought about her physical health. This time her face appeared more wrinkled than ever. Traces of facial cream still remained and it had more the pallor of a corpse than of a human being. Her cheeks were sunken and her eyes unrecognizable from before with dark rings around them and a vacant gaze. How could Wit have recognized her like this when before, her complexion had been so bright and fresh and there had been no wrinkles on her face? She had had no need of cosmetics to conceal, her eyes had been sparkling bright, her cheeks nice and full, and she had not needed to paint her lips red then as she did now. Love! It was no more than an illusion. Beauty and good looks were instruments to make men fall blindly in love, but in the end, nothing lasted; both love and good looks fell into decay.

Reun's hand gradually slipped from the mirror frame. Her neck gave way and her chin slumped against her chest. She staggered back to bed. But how could she sleep with the sound of men and women murmuring and whispering both above her and below? She tossed and turned restlessly in her misery. She could not get to sleep in this position and when she changed, she still could not. Eventually, she got up once more and wandered around until she was quite exhausted. What could she do to cure her misery and restlessness? The only way she had seen others use was drink. She would try it. Perhaps it would work. She tiptoed silently into Mae Choey's room where Mae Choey used to line up the glasses of whisky which the men had left unfinished. Reun secretly poured

some into a glass, drank as much as she could, and went back
to bed, her head spinning. Her body, which had been so
cold, gradually warmed up so that she fell asleep almost
immediately. Her brain, however, continued to work, con-
juring up a painful nightmare. In her dream, she saw Jitra sav-
agely beating her child. There was nothing she could do to
help because there was an iron gate in front of her. All she
could do was grab hold of the iron bars with her two hands,
her body trembling violently. The little child kept screaming
for help from her mother and Wit, who was standing at some
distance, but he just laughed with satisfaction when he saw
what Jitra was doing. She pulled Eet's fine hair and then
slapped her hard across the cheek, immediately silencing the
child. Reun screamed at the top of her voice and woke suddenly with a start. Her heart was pounding because of what
she had seen, but realizing it was only a dream, she gradually
calmed down. Just half a glass of whisky had given her such a
terrible nightmare. She tried to banish the dream from her
mind. Could Jitra really be so heartless? Jitra had had a good
education, so Wit had told her, and so, too, had Wit. Surely
he could not be so cruel as to stand back and watch Jitra slap
and beat his child as he had in her dream? It was, after all, just a
dream ... a dream she had had while her mind was in turmoil.

Reun did not sleep again. When daybreak came, she got
up quickly, washed, and dressed. Those who saw her com-
mented on her pale appearance. But instead of taking any
notice, she just got angry. Reun was always regarded as
unpredictable. She was no longer afraid of anyone or anything and was aggressive to anyone who upset her. Everyone
who had seen her since she got up was puzzled, including
Mae Choey.

'Where are you going?' she asked, seeing Reun dressed up
as if she was going out. 'Aren't you going to have something
to eat first?'

'No,' said Reun abruptly. She left the house and, in a highly agitated state, went straight round to see Mae Peu-ut and Nai Klin.

Twenty-four

EET did not want to go to school and was playing up. As soon as she saw her mother enter the room, her arms loaded with things, tears of laughter came to her eyes. She rushed over to her mother and grabbed her legs. She was all sweetness now.

'Mummy, you never come and see me. I miss you, Mummy.'

'Oh yes, that's very nice,' cried Mae Peu-ut. She was getting agitated and seemed to be looking for a cane. 'My goodness, she turns on the charm for her mother, all right. She's been playing up from the moment she woke up. She won't go to school. I've pleaded with her, I've threatened her, but she just won't listen. Look over there,' she said, pointing towards a shoe lying in front of a vase. 'She threw that slipper and nearly smashed the vase.' Nai Klin looked up and chuckled and then bent over the piece of wood he was paring. He earned his living making kites and catapults.

Reun knelt down and took hold of the child by the arms. 'Why aren't you going to school?' she asked, looking into the jet-black eyes which returned her gaze with an imploring look. 'Come on, then, tell Mummy.' Her darling child. She was counting the days to when her dear little girl would know only happiness. Mother and child would go their own separate ways. Eet would follow the same path as children who have a father to look after and care for them. As for her, she would soon be forgotten by her daughter. She would not remember who her real mother was. She would regard the woman who had raised her as her real mother.

Eet looked as if she was on the verge of tears because she thought her mother was going to make her go to school. 'I don't want to go, Mummy,' she replied. 'I want to stay with you.'

It was just what Reun wanted to hear. She did not want her child to go because she wanted to be with her as much as possible in the next two or three days before they were parted. 'All right then, I'll let you stay,' Reun said, sitting down with Eet and spreading out the things she had bought on the floor. 'But don't go running about outside, OK? The other day I saw you messing about in front of that Chinese fellow's shop. He'll come out and get you and then sell you.'

'I have to have my wits about me all the time,' Nai Klin complained. 'Once she found a satang in my cigarette box, and she was off in an instant to buy a lollipop while I was still bending over sticking the kite paper.'

'What did you do that for?' Reun asked, hoisting Eet up on to her lap. 'That's naughty. In future, if you want something to eat, you have to tell your father and ask him to buy it for you. Do you understand?' With her free hand, Reun passed a paper bag over to Mae Peu-ut, who had sat down opposite her. 'I was passing through Banglampu, so I stopped off to get some rambutans for you and Nai Klin. This is for Eet.'

In the other bag was a jar of candy which looked like pebbles, both in shape and colour. 'What have we got here, then?' she asked with a forced laugh, as she showed it to Eet.

'They're stones, aren't they?' said Eet. 'Why did you buy me a jar full of stones, Mummy?' She reached out for the jar with both hands and looked at the sweets in puzzlement.

Mae Peu-ut had never seen anything like it before, either. She leaned forward to take a closer look. 'Ooh yes. I thought they were real stones, too. Klin! Klin! Come and take a look at this. They're sweets, but they look like stones. They're clever, they are, those *farang*.'

Nai Klin was as curious as his wife. He put down his knife and the piece of bamboo and went over to have a look at Eet's sweets and to help open the jar. Mae Peu-ut thanked Reun for the rambutans, but she was really eager to know about the events of the previous evening.

'Who was that with you last night, Reun?' she asked when the opportunity arose.

'Eet's father,' Reun replied quietly, her head lowered so that her chin touched the child's hair. A strange expression came over her face when she spoke of Wit.

'There you are, Klin,' said Mae Peu-ut, slapping her thighs happily and laughing at her husband. 'I told you so. He's got the same face as Eet. Just like they came out of the same mould.'

'So that's your husband, then,' said Nai Klin thoughtlessly.

'Don't go thinking there's anything between us,' Reun said. 'He's from a wealthy, prominent family. He's got a wife and child. As for me, well, you know what I am.'

'You can tell from his appearance that he's not any old riff-raff,' Mae Peu-ut interjected. 'So he came to visit his kid, then, did he? I was going to ask you last night, but I didn't dare to, and then you left so quickly.' As she finished speaking, she stared at Reun's body as if she was thinking that such a body ought not to be able to get such a good husband as that gentleman last night.

'He's going to come and pick Eet up and look after her,' Reun replied wearily. She held Eet's hand and squeezed it gently.

Mae Peu-ut looked stunned. 'Oh my God! You don't mean it, do you? Oh Lord! What about me? I've looked after her since she was a baby. I've loved her as if she were my own,' she wailed, 'and now you're going to take her away.' She stared at Eet with a look of sadness and regret. Sadness, because she had raised the child and Eet was a dear little girl; and regret that she was losing the chance of earning a bit of money, because she was much more hard-up than before and Nai Klin's kite-making was not bringing in very much.

'What else can I do, Mae Peu-ut?' Reun mumbled, tears welling up in her eyes. 'I'm her real mother, so doesn't that count for more?' She gazed at her child, who sat, cheeks bulging with sweets, oblivious to what the adults were saying about her. She was picking out the pretty ones, examining them contentedly, as if they really were stones.

Up until then, Nai Klin had remained silent. 'It's difficult to say it, but her luck has changed and we shouldn't hold her back in hardship with us,' he said, unselfishly. 'If she stays with us, life will be tough for her. Her father loves her and he's well-off, so he'll be able to provide for her and offer her a happy future. All we have to offer are our hearts. It would be like cutting her off from a future. You're not looking so good these days, Reun. You look paler and thinner than before.'

'Yes, you're right,' Mae Peu-ut added. 'I was going to ask her when she came in why she looked so pale. Have you had anything to eat yet?'

Reun shook her head in reply. 'No, I'm not hungry. I don't want anything.'

'That's no good, now, Reun,' said Nai Klin. 'Try to force yourself to take even just a few mouthfuls to keep your strength up.' As he returned to where he had been sitting whittling away at the kite frame, he caught sight of a well-dressed middle-aged woman accompanied by a servant girl carrying a basket. Nai Klin's face fell as he turned to his wife. 'Peu-ut! The landlady's here.'

Before Mae Peu-ut had time to get up and go and greet her, the landlady had invited herself in and sat down with an arrogant look in her eyes. 'Am I going to get the rent today, then?' she demanded.

Mae Peu-ut wore an identical expression to her husband's. She hurriedly prepared the betel bowl and brought it in, but the landlady interrupted her. 'Don't bother. I've got quite enough betel of my own. It will be better if you just bring me the rent.'

'I'd be ever so grateful if you could give me until the fifteenth,' Mae Peu-ut replied hesitantly.

Reun sat and listened in silence, watching the arrogant manner of the owner. She thought back to the time when she was renting a room in Worajak with Samorn and the rent-collector had come asking for the outstanding money when Samorn had been ill. It was the same night that she had decided she would have to return to prostitution. Looking at Mae Peu-ut, she felt sorry for her, even though she knew that Mae Peu-ut was the sort of person who took advantage of her fellow human beings. She picked up her purse and took out a 10-baht note. 'Don't ask for any favours from her,' she said, passing the banknote to Mae Peu-ut. 'Give her this and she'll leave. Then perhaps she'll pay for someone to repair the leaks in the roof.'

Reun's words were full of anger. She felt that from now on there was nothing more to fear. She might just as well speak her mind. By keeping quiet, you simply let people trample all over you. The landlady stared at her angrily. She had opened her purse and taken the money but her hands were shaking with rage. She looked up. Seeing the maid who had accompanied her craning her neck to see whether there really were holes in the roof, she became even angrier. 'What do you think you're looking at?' she shouted. 'Just you wait.'

Both husband and wife heaved a sigh of relief and thanked Reun for helping them pay the rent. Mae Peu-ut made a great fuss of her and went out to buy her *kao tom* in her eagerness to please. Reun forced herself to swallow a few spoonfuls but that was all she could manage.

'What's the matter?' asked Mae Peu-ut, who sat watching her. 'You've hardly touched it.'

'I can't manage any more. I don't know what's the matter with me these days,' Reun grumbled.

'Take a break and look after yourself a bit,' Nai Klin advised. 'Your daughter's better now. There's no need to worry about sending us money like there was before.'

Reun didn't answer. She remained silent for some time. 'I'd like to come and be with Eet for a few days,' she said finally in a weary voice, 'because soon, her father will come and take her away.' Her heart sank as she spoke of separation from her daughter.

'Come and stay here, Reun,' said Mae Peu-ut quite genuinely. 'There's no need to feel embarrassed. It's perfectly all right. It's a bit small inside. You and Eet can sleep in the inner net and I'll come out and sleep in the outer one.'

'I can sleep anywhere,' said Reun. 'The kitchen would be fine.'

The invitation was just what Reun wanted, so that she could be close to her daughter. It was agreed that from that night on Reun would stay at Mae Peu-ut's house and help to look after her daughter. She took her to a dressmaker to get several new dresses made with the money that Wit had given her. Now, at least, Jitra would not be in a position to look down on Eet for being dirty and inadequately clothed. All the time, however, Reun's condition got steadily worse. She had a chronic cough and fever, and she had a pain in her chest when she breathed. She gritted her teeth and told no one of her condition. Seeing her daughter at close quarters, she felt sad one moment, because the child was going to live with Wit, and glad at others that her daughter would have the happiness she had always wanted for her.

Time passed until the appointed day came. Reun hurried over to Mae Choey's house to wait for Wit as arranged. At about nine o'clock that night, Wit arrived. The broad smile on his face indicated that nothing would prevent him from taking his child to live with him.

Wit made no immediate reference to his child as he approached. On the contrary, he greeted Reun with surprise. 'Reun, you've been ill again since I last saw you, haven't you? Your face looks so pale.'

Reun smiled sadly. 'No, I'm fine,' she replied and then changed the subject. 'Have you sorted things out with Khun Jitra yet, about having Eet to live with you?'

Wit was still staring at Reun's face with shock and pity. Ever since the day they had reached an agreement about the child, Wit had felt more and more sympathy for all the hardship and suffering Reun had undergone. He admired her strength and resolution. There were not many girls like her. He sat down on a chair facing her. 'Yes,' he said. 'I've sorted things out with Jitra.'

'Is she willing?' Reun asked doubtfully.

'I'll tell you the truth and then you won't need to go wondering about it any more. Jitra was very sad and upset to learn that my involvement with you went as far as having a child. She had hoped to have a husband who was pure and untainted by past affairs. It's true, what you told me before. I tried to explain to her fully that what had happened to my life, to yours, and the child's was nobody's fault because some powers beyond us had made us all the victims of sin. Out of a hundred men, I told her, you'd only find ten that had never been involved with a woman, and even then I wouldn't guarantee whether those ten were sound in body or not. Apart from that, I told Jitra about all your difficulties. Eventually, she made up her mind and told me she was willing for me to bring the child to live with us because she loved me and was happy to set aside her feelings about her because she is of the same blood as the man she loves. Then she told me to beg you to allow her and me the opportunity between us to repay your goodness in some way. Jitra asked me to ask you again about me renting a house for you, Reun,' Wit added after he had outlined the understanding he and his wife had reached.

'From all you've told me, I would like to thank Khun Jitra for all her kindness. What else should I want from her? I don't want anything from her. Nothing at all,' Reun said, with a bitter look on her face.

Wit was silent, not knowing what to say. Reun would not accept anything from him in return. 'I'll come and pick the child up tomorrow afternoon at about three or four o'clock,' he said.

'Yes,' said Reun. 'I shall be there, too.' Then, with tears in her eyes, she looked at him and spoke in a trembling voice. 'Wit, I'm giving her over into your care. I believe you will take good care of her.' Then she was silent once more.

'Don't worry, Reun. I guarantee you that I shan't let her endure any trouble or hardship. But what about you, Reun? I fear you're not well. Call the doctor round.'

Reun waved her hand. 'No, I'm fine.' No sooner had she spoken than she felt an almost uncontrollable urge to cough, but she tried to control it. After some time, she spoke. 'Go home now. Don't hang around here.'

Wit, however, would not just leave at Reun's behest. It was as if something were making him feel a sense of sadness and longing at leaving the girl he had once loved and been close to. He wanted to sit near her and look closely at the face which had once been so full and bright and the body which had once lain in his arms, but which now no longer retained any trace of beauty. Her physical appearance had deteriorated quite visibly. Her voice, once so sweet and gentle, was now weak and hoarse. Reun made him ponder—ponder too much—on all the beauty and illusion he had encountered. She was a prostitute, it was true, but she had a heart beyond compare. Yet it remained difficult for anyone to see the goodness in her. The world would always condemn her as a prostitute, a brazen woman who sold sex for a living.

Twenty-five

THE following day, Reun dragged her weary body round to Mae Peu-ut and Nai Klin's house to tell them that Wit would be coming to collect Eet that afternoon. Their feelings were inevitably in a turmoil, a mixture of anticipation and sadness, and they took it in turns to hold the child for the last time. A sweet little girl like Eet would never be deprived of love, especially from the person who had cared for her and fed her since she was tiny, to the point of almost feeling it was her own child. Mae Peu-ut was on the verge of tears. She did not feel like doing anything. Nai Klin was putting on a brave face. He had stopped whittling away at the wooden kite frame and sat staring vacantly against the wall, hugging his knees with a *pakaoma* draped round his shoulders. Eet did not pay much attention. She did not even know whether it had anything to do with her or not. All she did know was that everyone was being very nice to her today. They were not scolding her as they usually did. She could throw Fat Mummy's betel box as far as she liked and she did not get into trouble as she had previously when she had done the same thing. She ran about making a lot of noise and Nai Klin said nothing. When she was worn out, she came and sat down and watched Thin Mummy pick up the new clothes she had had made for her and pile them up in a large piece of square cloth.

'Mummy, why are you putting my clothes in that cloth?' Eet asked, tugging at her mother's arm.

'I'm packing for you,' Reun replied in a trembling voice. She could not look her little daughter in the eyes.

'Why do you have to pack them? What about that one?' she asked, pointing to a blouse that had been put to one side. 'Why haven't you put that one in?'

'I kept that one out for you to wear this afternoon,' her mother said.

'Why do I have to wear a new blouse? It'll make Fat Mummy cross.' She glanced across at Mae Peu-ut, who always used to shout at her if she tried to put on a new blouse.

'I won't shout at you today,' said Mae Peu-ut, wiping away a tear with the edge of her *pa taep* as she disappeared into the kitchen.

Reun finished packing her daughter's clothes. At about half-past two that afternoon, when the sun had gone down a little, Reun bathed her daughter, inwardly fretting all the time that the time was approaching when she would be parted from her child. Let me bath you just one last time, my treasure. When you go to live with your father, you'll be surrounded by servants. But I wonder whether they will bath and dress you properly. Perhaps they'll neglect you or not look after you properly at mealtimes and bedtime. My darling child, don't you know to even look me straight in the eyes, so you'll remember who your real mother is? Leaving you like this, I feel as if my heart is being torn out of my body.

Reun dressed her daughter up in the new blouse and skirt, powdered her face, and combed her fine hair so that it would look tidy. Then she let her go and sit outside. Reun went into the kitchen to speak to Mae Peu-ut, who was in the middle of putting the food she had prepared in the cupboard. 'Mae Peu-ut, please see Eet off when Khun Wit comes. I can't do it myself. I feel as if I'm being torn apart.' Tears streamed down her face.

Mae Peu-ut's eyes were red. She nodded. Reun was sobbing as she spoke but she was quite emphatic. 'If he asks about me, please tell him I'm not in.' She went outside and hugged her child tightly to her, sobbing with an intense feeling of sadness and longing. She looked closely at Eet's face. Eet looked as if she was about to burst into tears without understanding why. She buried her head against her mother's breast and remained there in silence, almost causing Reun to collapse on the spot. She kissed her daughter's tiny hands, her cheeks, her chin, and all over her face, not worried about her face which she had made up to greet Eet's father. Sobbing more violently, Reun hugged her little girl and would not let go, until Nai Klin, who had been sitting outside keeping a look-out, called out in a trembling voice, 'Here he comes. He's coming.' She set her child down from her lap and got up. Bending over, she kissed Eet again on the head for the last time. Then she walked away, crying, to hide herself in the kitchen.

Reun heard Wit speaking to Nai Klin and Mae Peu-ut in a low voice and then she heard the child crying as if she was refusing to go with the strange man who was her father. The sound of her child's crying caused Reun to collapse in despair on the floor, as if a needle had pierced her heart. It was as if those cries were accusing her of not loving her darling child. Gradually, the sound faded away. Her dear daughter was gone. Reun was silent, in a daze, like someone unconscious or lifeless.

'They've gone now,' said Mae Peu-ut, entering the kitchen. 'Come on out now, Reun. Dear me, she was so nice. She gave me another 20 baht. Hey, Reun! Reun, what's the matter?' She was alarmed to see Reun slumped over in the kitchen. She went over and touched her. She felt as cold as ice. 'Klin! Come here, quickly,' she cried with a shrill scream. 'I don't know what the matter is with Reun.'

Nai Klin rushed to her assistance. He found the medicine and between them they brought her out of the kitchen. As she gradually came round, Reun tried to sit up. She coughed violently a few times and spat into the spitoon. There was blood in it. 'Oh, good grief,' cried Mae Peu-ut immediately. 'You're coughing blood. It's no good. You must look after yourself.'

'That's not blood, Mae Peu-ut,' Reun protested hoarsely. 'Why be so alarmed? I'm perfectly all right.' She forced herself to try to act as if there was nothing wrong with her and she was not in any pain. She controlled herself so as not to appear any worse than this and got up as if to go outside.

Mae Peu-ut stopped her, for by now, Reun was feverish. 'Where are you going? You're not completely better yet. You're only just on the mend.'

'Let me go,' Reun said crying. 'Let me go. I can't stay.'

'You've got to be brave now, Reun,' Nai Klin said, trying to bring her to her senses. 'Your child has gone, it's true, but she'll be happy. Don't go out wandering around now. You're not well. Lie down and rest here. Khun Wit said that tomorrow morning he would come round again to see you at 11 o'clock and wanted you to wait. He's so good, you know. I was carrying Eet out for him, but he said there was no need and that he would take her himself. He seems to be really fond of her. If he loves his child like that, there's nothing for us to worry about any more.'

Between them, the couple restrained Reun from going out and tried to calm her down. They made food for her and put her to bed. All night, she tossed and turned in a feverish condition. She coughed frequently and thought she had the same symptoms as Samorn. Exhausted, she drifted off to sleep early that evening. She dreamed that Samorn was standing in front of her. 'Have you forgotten me, Reun?' she asked 'Are you going to live with me?' she cried in a shrill voice that was mixed with laughter. Reun woke with a start, her body shaking. 'Morn was trying to follow her, beckoning from the top of the mosquito net. And it was not only 'Morn. Images of her mother and father revolved before her eyes. Delirious, she reached upwards with her hands until she heard a startled Mae Peu-ut and Nai Klin come to see her.

'Is that you, 'Morn?' Have you come to see the little one? She's gone. Oh no, my little darling,' Reun cried, reaching out with her arms, 'come back to me.'

'Reun! Reun!' cried Mae Peu-ut taking her by the hands and calling her to her senses.

Reun opened her reddened eyes and looked at her. She laughed, a chilling laugh that made Mae Peu-ut's hair stand on end. 'Is that you, Mae Peu-ut? Aren't you pleased, then? You've raised Eet since she was little and now she is going to be happy.'

'Yes, I'm pleased, Reun. Calm down now and lie down.' Mae Peu-ut made an effort to comfort Reun. She lifted a glass of water to Reun's parched lips. 'Here, drink some water, Reun. Get some sleep and try to calm yourself. Khun Wit is coming to see you tomorrow.'

Reun smiled weakly when she heard the name of the one she loved so much and she did as she was told. Gradually, she came to her senses, but the image of Samorn and her parents remained before her eyes. She lay there restless, thinking of her child and the last time she had seen Wit. Now Eet would be sleeping contentedly on a soft bed. When Reun thought of all these comforts, she smiled and laughed softly. When she thought of her own suffering and sorrow, she cried. It was like this until daybreak.

The next morning, Mae Peu-ut and Nai Klin felt less alarmed because Reun had got up and was sitting down as if there was nothing wrong with her. It was as if she were getting ready to meet Wit. But no. When the time Wit had arranged to see her approached, Reun gave instructions to tell him that she was not in because she did not want to have anything more to do with him. When they heard this, Mae Peu-ut and Nai Klin were saddened and felt sorry for her. Before, they had looked down on her as a prostitute. Now, they saw that, even if she was a prostitute, she was purer in heart and more single-minded than anyone they had ever met.

Wit arrived at the appointed time. He was pleased to be coming to see Reun. He felt sorry for her and could not bear the thought of not coming today. He was planning to take her to see a doctor and to beg her to go and live in a house that he had already arranged to rent for her.

'Is Reun in?' he asked Nai Klin, who was sitting alone in front of the house.

Reun heard Wit's voice in the distance as she lay there waiting. She felt suddenly alarmed and her heart sank. His voice was soft and gentle. It had a strange power which compelled her to get up from where she lay. Slowly, and very weakly, she propped herself up in a sitting position. She wanted to see once more the face of the dear husband of her dreams. She gritted her teeth and inched nearer the red floral curtain which hung in the middle of the room. But then she collapsed again, exhausted. She propped herself up and stretched out a hand, which was no more than skin and bones and grabbed the curtain tightly. She gazed at Wit through hazy eyes. She could see him clearly. My darling, you've taken pity on me and come to see me. Her hand clutched the curtain tightly and pulled it towards her. Reun smiled through her tears … smiled with happiness. When she saw Wit about to leave, her hand gradually released its grip on the curtain and let it fall against her. Her face was pale but bore the trace of a happy smile. Slowly, she slumped weak and exhausted against the edge of the curtain.

Mae Peu-ut emerged from the kitchen carrying an earthenware bowl full of hot water. She was intending to take it to Reun to drink, but when she saw Wit talking to Nai Klin, she dared not enter the room. As soon as Wit had gone out of the door, Mae Peu-ut carefully carried the bowl in.

Out of sight, Nai Klin had turned away from the handsome figure of Wit and was coming back. Suddenly, his hair stood on end. The sound of the bowl slipping from Mae Peu-ut's hand made a loud, resounding crash, a sharp, frightening sound. It was a sign of sorrow. A sign that announced that the pure soul of a woman whose goodness the world rewarded with injustice had slipped away from that pitiful body. Nothing remained except the soft echo of a whisper, 'Ah, sin it is, that has to support virtue'.

*   *   *

Who would have thought that the story two fellow travellers had mentioned in fun to pass the time on the train would end in such tears?

Glossary

Ba	Aunt; term of address for older women.
chao	Royal title; a person bearing that title.
chao khun	Conferred title, similar to 'His Lordship'; a person bearing that title.
chao phraya	Highest rank of conferred nobility; a person with that rank.
farang	Westerner.
gaeng liang	Type of Thai curry or stew.
ja	Syllable added at the end of a sentence to convey a sense of informality or intimacy.
Jataka	Collection of approximately 500 stories telling of former incarnations of the Buddha.
ka	Syllable added at the end of a sentence by female speakers to indicate polite or formal speech.
kamnan	District headman.
kanom	Sweets, dessert.
kao tom	Rice porridge.
kao tom pla	Rice porridge with fish.
Khun	Polite title occurring with the personal name of both males and females.
khun nang	Conferred title; a person bearing that title.
khun phra	Conferred title; a person bearing that title.
khunying	Conferred title, similar to 'Lady'; a person bearing that title.
khunnai	Conferred title; a person bearing that title.
kloo-ay boo-ut chee	Bananas boiled in coconut cream.
Lung	Uncle; term of address for old men.
Mae	Term of address for women.
mae sri kao pii ling	Traditional Thai game.

mom	Title given to the wife of a prince; a person bearing that title.
Na	Aunt; term of address for old women.
nang yeepun	Japanese film.
naem	Shredded pork which has been salted and slightly fermented.
pakaoma	Check-patterned cloth used by men as a loincloth.
pa lai	Patterned Thai-style skirt.
pa nung	Thai-style skirt.
pa sin	Thai-style skirt.
pa taep	Cloth worn by women to cover their breasts.
phaya	Non-hereditary title conferred by the king, usually on government officials; a person bearing that title.
Phra Aphaimani	A Thai literary classic, named after the hero.
pinphat	Thai orchestra, consisting of drums, oboe, xylophone, and gongs.
pla chorn	Type of fish: snakehead mullet.
pu yai	Village headman.
sakae	Small tree, commonly used for firewood; *Combretum quadrangulare* (Combretaceae).
sa-noh	Tall marsh plant used for making charcoal; *Sesbania roxburghii* (Leguminosae).
sara	Vowel.
satang	Unit of Thai currency; 1 baht = 100 satang.
Songkran	Thai New Year, which falls in mid-April.
Ta	Grandfather; term of address for old men.
towkay	Rich Chinese.
wahn	Sweet (adj.); often used as a girl's nickname.
ya hom	Traditional Thai medicine.
Yai	Grandmother; term of address for old women.

Other Oxford Paperbacks for readers interested in South-East Asia, past and present

Titles marked with an asterisk have restricted rights.